Felix Economakis is a highly experienced chartered psychologist, clinical hypnotherapist and master NLP practitioner, with his own private clinic in London. He is known to BBC3 viewers as the psychologist on *The Panic Room* and *Freaky Eaters*, where he used clinical hypnosis and more traditional psychological approaches to cure people of their phobias and food problems.

Praise for this book:

'A practical, inspiring and incredibly useful guide to living.'

– Tania Ahsan, editor of *Kindred Spirit*

'Will give you all the tools to develop deep-rooted self-esteem and self-confidence.'

– Dr Harinder Mann, Lecturer in entrepreneurship

TAKE CHARGE
OF YOUR LIFE
WITH

NLP

FELIX ECONOMAKIS

Vermilion
LONDON

1 3 5 7 9 10 8 6 4 2

Published in 2011 by Vermilion, an imprint of Ebury Publishing
Ebury Publishing is a Random House Group company

The Random House Group Limited Reg. No. 954009
Addresses for companies within the Random House Group can be found at
www.randomhouse.co.uk

A CIP catalogue record for this book is available from the British Library

The Random House Group Limited supports The Forest Stewardship Council
(FSC®), the leading international forest certification organisation. Our books
carrying the FSC label are printed on FSC® certified paper. FSC is the only
forest certification scheme endorsed by the leading environmental organisations,
including Greenpeace. Our paper procurement policy can be found at
www.randomhouse.co.uk/environment

Printed and bound by CPI Group (UK) Ltd, Croydon, CR0 4YY

Cover author photograph © Laurence Cendrowicz

ISBN 9780091939731

Copies are available at special rates for bulk orders. Contact the sales
development team on 020 7840 8487 for more information.

To buy books by your favourite authors and register for offers, visit
www.randomhouse.co.uk

The information in this book has been compiled by way of general guidance in
relation to the specific subjects addressed, but is not a substitute and not to be
relied on for medical, healthcare, pharmaceutical or other professional advice on
specific circumstances and in specific locations. Please consult your GP before
changing, stopping or starting any medical treatment. So far as the author is
aware the information given is correct and up to date as at September 2011.
Practice, laws and regulations all change, and the reader should obtain up to date
professional advice on any such issues. The author and publishers disclaim, as
far as the law allows, any liability arising directly or indirectly from the use, or
misuse, of the information contained in this book.

Contents

For Crissy, Lara and JJ

Acknowledgements

Special thank you to my marvellous editor, Louise Coe, for her superhuman patience, advice and meticulous care. It takes a special person to have the dedication to keep rereading material numerous times with fresh eyes while analysing new concepts, relevance, coherency, spelling mistakes and syntax all at the same time. I was very lucky to have her and this is a far better book as a consequence.

Thank you also to my long-suffering wife who had to put up with my mental absences in the course of writing this book. On countless occasions we would be talking and something in our discussion would strike a chord with me. My eyes would take on a faraway look, then I'd rush to my laptop and use that example in my work and she'd sigh and get on with things. Thank you, sweetheart, for your patience.

Thank you to my two lovely children for giving me the opportunity to watch and learn from them, providing me with my own private psychological laboratory to refine my theories.

Foreword

I first came across NLP in 1990, thanks to Anthony Robbins' book *Unlimited Power*. I had heard of the subconscious mind before, but it all sounded a bit 'woo-woo' and weird. This was different. As an engineer by trade, I loved the pragmatic step-by-step techniques that promised to change my life. More importantly, they worked for me! By 1993 I had decided that I wanted to teach NLP to as many people as possible, and since then I have trained tens of thousands of people from Hawaii and LA to London, the Netherlands and Israel.

It has been, and continues to be, an amazing journey. Over the years I have witnessed the incredible power of NLP techniques to assist people in changing their lives. I have seen people use NLP to heal family rifts, fix broken marriages, banish phobias and post-traumatic stress disorder, as well as become hugely successful in business.

I first met Felix Economakis in 2005, on my NLP master practitioner certification course. As a trainer it is always a thrill to see one of your previous delegates become so successful, and a great honour to be asked to write the foreword for their book.

Felix has taken a unique angle on NLP, integrating it with his expertise in clinical psychology. He fully embraces the way NLP works with the subconscious mind and shows people how to work with it directly. This millennium has been described by many as the millennium of the mind. In this book, Felix tells you how you can make your own mind work for you.

We are all given the most amazing, powerful gift at birth – a subconscious mind. When we get to the age of about five, six or seven we develop a conscious mind, and, for many of us, the path to loosing contact with and trust in our subconscious mind begins. Unfortunately we have never had an instruction manual or user guide for working with our two minds ... until now! In *Take Charge of Your Life With NLP*, Felix eloquently describes how your subconscious mind works and then gives you simple, yet powerful techniques to regain the connection and communication you once had. These processes will enable anyone to unlock the power of their subconscious mind.

By following Felix's instructions and completing the exercises, you can expect to experience a number of profound changes in your life. Firstly your intuition will skyrocket – as it is your subconscious mind that passes on the infinite information around you to your conscious mind through what we call 'intuition' or 'gut feelings'. You will also begin to experience a greater emotional richness in your life, as your subconscious mind is the home of our emotions. Learning to pay attention to these feelings will bring back balance, joy and a sense of fun. Finally, Felix gives you powerful processes to heal inner conflicts and gain insight in how to heal conflicts that you may have with others in your life. This will bring a sense of inner peace and calm.

To have all of this, and more, all you need to do is read Felix's words and do the processes he describes.

Have a wonderful time getting to know your unconscious!

David Shephard

President Of The American Board Of NLP
Certified Master Trainer of NLP
Certified Master Trainer of NLP Coaching
Certified Master Trainer of Hypnosis
Certified Master Trainer of Time Line Therapy®
www.davidshephard.com

Introduction

'Ninety per cent of the world's woe comes from people not knowing themselves, their abilities, their frailties and even their real virtues. Most of us go almost all the way through life as complete strangers to ourselves.'

Sidney J. Harris,
American journalist, 1917–1986

DESPITE THE FACT THAT HUMANS HAVE THE intelligence to land men on the moon, construct huge telescopes that can peer into deep space, and theorise about dark matter, most of us don't really have a good understanding of what makes us tick. We often find ourselves making the same silly mistakes over and over in our daily lives. But why is this?

Why, for instance, do some doctors smoke, despite knowing exactly how dire the consequences are for their health? Or why do we lie awake at night, worrying unduly about things, even when we've been through the same situations countless times before? Or why do we go for the same type of partner time and time again, only for our friends to say 'I told you so' after the inevitable break-up, to which we sheepishly reply, *'I know, I know...'*

Even professors of psychology are not immune to such influences. To quote one such professor: 'Why [do] I succumb to well-documented psychological biases even though I'm acutely aware of them.'[1]

As for me, when both of my young children were babies, in their first year they invariably kept waking up several times a night crying (and the best my wife and I could have hoped for on a good night was four or five hours' kip). So why couldn't I make myself go to bed before midnight, even though I knew I would benefit from more sleep?

Going against your 'better judgement' is infuriating, puzzling and bewildering. It can also be expensive in terms of health, wealth and time. And it seems we are all prone to it to some degree or other. But you don't need to keep repeating these kinds of patterns. If you spend some time discovering what's really going on, you could do something about it rather than squandering all that precious time and energy.

So what drives your behaviour?

As so much of what we understand about our environment is mediated through our conscious mind, it may come as a surprise to you to learn that, more often than most of us are aware of, much of our decisions are actually made by a part of ourselves that few of us ever think about – the subconscious.

Our conscious mind is our rational thinking mind and it helps us to make more logical and objective decisions, based

---

1 David Buss – see http://www.independent.co.uk/life-style/health-and-families/features/beyond-analysis-inside-the-minds-of-the-worlds-top-psychologists-1797650.html

on clinical cost–benefit analysis. That means we might choose not to take a second piece of cake as we have consciously decided that the pleasure of eating it is outweighed by the time we would have to spend in the gym to work off the calories.

Our subconscious mind is our more emotional mind, which guides our decisions based on our emotional values. Some of these emotional values will be biologically driven (e.g. universal responses such as our fear response in the face of something unknown and scary), while other values will be based on how we feel about things and experiences around us. So using the cake example above, we might reach for the second piece of cake, as our subconscious is telling us that eating it will fill an emotional need.

It's worthwhile to mention here that the 'unconscious mind' is an umbrella term that refers to all the multitude of functions and processes involved in life, such as breathing and digestion, which do not concern us here. The subconscious mind is a subset of the unconscious mind and the part more involved with our emotions and feelings.

Furthermore, the conscious mind is also associated more with the logical, rational and analytical left-hemisphere, while the subconscious mind is more associated with the creative, imaginative and emotional right-hemisphere. Hence the phrase 'left-brained' for very analytical people and 'right-brained' for those intensely artistic types.

All the decisions and choices we make in our lives are governed by either our conscious mind or our subconscious mind. The same choices facing us can be decided on rational and pragmatic terms or decided in terms of our feelings and emotions. Some people choose their partners based on very practical considerations (income, status, location) with a view to ensuring their lives are easier and more secure, and some people choose their partners purely for emotional reasons, reasons which if anything have ended up making their lives infinitely harder and more complicated, by choosing to have long-distance relationships, for example, or to hook up with people whose lives are in a mess and being drawn in to help them pick up the pieces.

Emotions, therefore, can lead us to make decisions independent of any considerations of logic, pragmatism or usefulness.

Sometimes logic and feelings can match up well (e.g., buying furniture that is aesthetically pleasing and useful and within our budget). Other times they can mismatch completely and we do things against our better judgement (buying stuff we can't afford, we don't need and we don't use).

But which mind is stronger?

Imagine a huge iceberg. The tip sticking out of the water is equivalent to your conscious thinking mind. Underneath the water, and invisible to the observer, lies the majority of the iceberg, which equates to your subconscious or emotional part of your mind. It's this greater mass that is actually moving the iceberg. The irony is the tip thinks (if icebergs can think!) that it's the one who is in control. Just like the iceberg, we may pride ourselves as being intelligent, independent thinkers, on our 'reason', yet the truth is that we are much more emotional creatures than we are rational ones, and it is our subconscious, emotional mind that drives most of our behaviour.

Have you ever rejected a supermarket own brand product in favour of an identical more expensive branded version without really wondering why? In this case, your subconscious, emotional mind has been influenced by advertising. Advertising sells on associating certain desirable emotions to certain products, rather than on any scientific evidence. Have you noticed how most chocolate adverts tend to have an attractive, slim female experiencing rapture while eating a bar? Or, in the case of crisps or alcohol, a *group* of young, slim, attractive (and invariably multiracial) people eating and drinking those brands while also looking as if they're having the time of their lives? Logically there is little correlation between washboard stomachs and the kinds of people who eat and drink a lot of crisps, chocolate and beer, but the advertising industry spends several billion pounds a year on trying to subconsciously convince us of this link.

Why are advertisers willing to invest so much money in creating such unrealistic and artificial emotional associations? Because their research has already convinced them of the fact that most of our decisions are not made rationally. Advertisers are trying to cash in on the fact that most of us suffer an information and choice overload and cannot think consciously about every small decision in our life, with the result that we tend to operate on subconscious autopilot. Advertisers want to influence that subconscious autopilot to buy their clients' products. But never fear – over the course of this book, I can going to show you how to understand and influence your subconscious mind, so you have greater freedom of choice when making decisions.

That the subconscious mind is responsible for running most of our behaviour may not be news to you. That particular information has been out there for a while. But, given the tremendous impact of your subconscious mind on your life, just how well do you know your subconscious? If you have been feeling like your life has been like riding a horse that is careering out of control, it's likely that you're not in touch with this part of your mind. Throughout the pages of this book, I will give you some simple yet highly effective tools so that you can take the horse by the reins and steer it in the direction you want. After all, what's at stake here is more than just being drawn to choosing a branded good over the cheaper supermarket version. That's all small fry. Your subconscious mind heavily influences, for instance:

- what you habitually focus on in your life
- your level of self-confidence and self-belief
- your decision-making strategies
- the kinds of relationships to which you are drawn
- your level of emotional and mental health.

These, in turn, impact on the type of job and career you enter, how you perform in it (e.g. do you think you are a fraud and so consistently avoid promotions?), how you get on in both private and professional relationships, how you understand and parent your children, your outlook on the world and life in general.

Clearly, there are real massive benefits to working with our subconscious mind, yet for the most part most people's efforts to do so have been limited to a bit of formal hypnosis or listening to a few subliminal audiotapes or binaural beat sound waves or whatever. More often than not, the whole area of working with the subconscious mind has just been relegated to the 'important but don't know what to do about it' filing cabinet in our mind. What a waste.

Give our general ignorance about the subject, this reaction is understandable, but it is the aim of this book to shed some light on this hugely important part of ourselves, so that we may improve our decisions, our behaviour, our thoughts and our overall well-being.

One more thing: you may not be suffering from any particular psychological ailment per se, but instead be experiencing a more existential restlessness, as if something is missing. Many people express this as a desire to 'get to know themselves better' or 'find out who they are' (to 'Know Thyself' in the words of the Oracle of Delphi). Once again, getting to know your subconscious mind is the key here. The Oracle might as well have said 'Know your subconscious mind' because to 'know thyself' is really about knowing the 'unknown' part of us about which we are not conscious or aware of.

There are people who enter my consulting rooms having struggled for decades with fears, phobias, addictions or even psychosomatic problems and in just the space of a few short sessions (sometimes even just one or two), experience a massive, sometimes complete, change in their lives. Why should something that seemed so difficult then end up being relatively easy to resolve? I believe it's easy when you know where to apply the maximum leverage. NLP, or neurolinguistic programming, is one such way of making big changes in your life with the minimum effort and the maximum impact.

For those readers unfamiliar with NLP, this rather scary-sounding title refers to the use of language (the 'linguistic' part of NLP) to create desired changes in our brain and nervous system, our neurology, in other words, which is where the 'neuro' part of NLP comes from. For any change in our behaviour to become permanent, the pathways in our brain needs to be rewired and we achieve that by changing the language that we use to describe us and the world around us.

There's even a metaphor to describe the way we perceive the world, which you'll already be very familiar with. You've heard of someone being a 'glass half full' or a 'glass half empty' kind of person? The point is that there is exactly the same amount of liquid involved – how the amount is described makes all the difference. People who see the glass half full are said to be optimists; on the other hand, half-empty types are generally pessimistic, even cynical, seeing what they don't have, rather than what they're already got.

If you're a 'half-empty' person and want to see things in a sunnier way, you can do that by changing the way you describe the world and by doing that you use language, the linguistic part of NLP. Language in NLP can be used to create change directly through formal therapeutic techniques or indirectly through hypnotic language patterns and metaphors that work directly with your subconscious mind.

The 'reprogramming' part of NLP simply refers to the notion of reprogramming outdated and unhelpful thinking patterns with more useful and resourceful ones. It will probably come as no surprise to you that NLP practitioners have taken the analogy of software updates and reprogramming from the world of computers.

I can personally vouch for the effect of these approaches in my life.

Growing up, I was rather shy and had relatively low-self esteem, but, as an adult, I adopted some of the NLP approaches I outline in this book, which led to a quantum-leap improvement in my life. Previously I had always gone for jobs I was overqualified for and went for partners who were not at all right for me (as I did not think my ideal type of woman would want someone like me). As I learnt to manage myself with these same techniques, I started taking more risks. These included performing therapy in front of TV cameras, trusting myself to deal with all the challenges inherent in starting one's own business or in writing this book, and meeting, falling in love with and marrying a beautiful and intelligent woman. It was as if a magic wand had been waved, although instead of working in a flash, it took a few weeks of practice for these new habits to sink in and become second nature.

You too can have the experience of such a seeming magic wand effect on your life but it does require a similar modest investment of your time.

How NLP Will Help You

The information contained within this book uses NLP techniques to help you work better with your subconscious mind, allowing you to have:

- a greater and more accurate understanding of your personality and aspects of your behaviour that you currently find confusing and puzzling
- an overall improvement and freedom in the way you feel about yourself, with greater tolerance and self-acceptance and the feelings of being more at peace within yourself
- a healthier relationship with YOU. In essence you will be

working more with yourself rather than against, leading you to feel more in control of your actions and your life

- A general increase in your self-confidence, self-esteem and even an improvement in your relationships with others.

In addition, throughout this book there are numerous quick self-help techniques so you can either nip some old problem habits in the bud before they develop, or minimise them if you realise they have sneaked up on you.

This book is broken into six chapters.

Chapter 1 explains the subconscious mind and shows which of these aspects of the mind are responsible for undesirable behaviours that you or others around you may be experiencing.

Chapter 2 explains some of the reasons why we have developed poor relationships with our subconscious minds, ending up in the predicaments that many of us find ourselves in.

Chapter 3 addresses how to manage your 'inner child' aspect and Chapter 4 focuses on dealing with some of the typical problems caused by inner-child conflicts and how you can resolve them.

Chapter 5 focuses on working with 'parts', specifically the main types of problems caused by fears, addictions and psychosomatic problems, which are driven by soldier parts, pleasure-seeking parts and engineer parts. They can be seen as hampering you and your progress towards self-confidence and -esteem, but as I will show, they are essentially trying to help. It's up to your 'inner adult' to direct them better.

Please note: while some of you may be tempted to skip to the chapters that focus on the kinds of behaviours that you want to address immediately, it is still best to read all of chapters 3, 4 and 5 because of the overlap of the sphere of influence between the inner-child aspect and parts. In other words, the answers you may be looking for in one chapter may be present themselves in another. It will also provide a more rounded view of how your subconscious mind operates.

The final chapter asks you to consider the choice of paths you wish to pursue and build on to create the kind of life you desire.

There are many books out there promising a quick fix and 'instant' high self-esteem. I really don't see how they can deliver something lasting because I truly believe that developing a real core healthy self-esteem means cultivating a relationship with your subconscious mind, getting to know it, learning and meeting its needs, earning its trust by actions, as well as allowing for mishaps on the learning curve caused by trial and error. And this takes time. You would not expect someone you've been on just one date to trust you enough to marry you instantly. Marriage is a big commitment and a big investment. Your date needs time to trust you. Your relationship with your subconscious mind is no different. You are making an investment and, like most investments, this yields rewards over time rather than right away. Trust me on this point that, after working with thousands of people on this subject, all investments you do make here will provide life-changing returns.

1 Getting to Know Your Subconscious Mind

'Know thyself.'
– Oracle of Delphi

IMAGINE THAT I'M A DIRECTOR OF A BUSINESS AND I HAVE a vice-president who actually makes most of the daily decisions and runs the administration and maintenance of my office. If someone were to ask me 'who runs my business?' it would be inaccurate of me to dismiss my vice-president as just 'staff' and reply, 'I run the business', as in truth my VP runs it more than I do.

It is similar with your conscious and subconscious mind. When most people think of their personality, they tend to identify almost exclusively with their conscious mind, but your subconscious plays an even bigger role.

So the first thing I'd like you to take on board is the idea that you share your body with another part of you that has its own distinct personality – its own outlook on life, its own agenda, its own prejudices, even its own sense of pride. Moreover, this other personality in you has a different set of needs to yours and different ways of communicating those needs.

It comes as a shock to most people to learn that you can hurt your subconscious mind's feelings, just as you could a real person's. For them, it's akin to learning that they've hurt the feelings of their mobile phone. The subconscious mind tends to be viewed as just a mechanism that regulates our breathing, digestion, sleep systems and so forth – a very sophisticated one, but ultimately a mindless automaton much the same as our laptop or mobile phone.

But trust me; there's a lot, lot more to it than that. In over ten years of working at this kind of level, I can assure you that I've observed that our conscious mind can insult and offend our subconscious mind, even hurt its pride and our subconscious mind can retreat in injured resentment. It's just like seeing a real-life couple for couples counselling whereby, as a result of their relationship, one partner has become hurt, sad, despairing, depressed, mistrustful or resentful about the other.

The second thing therefore that I'd like you to now take on board is that you have a *relationship* with your subconscious mind, just like your relationship to anyone else to whom you are very attached. Conscious and subconscious minds argue and bicker, just like real couples do or just like parents row with their children. By 'couple' I am not just referring to spouses or romantic relationships, but any combination of two people in a close relationship.

You argue with your parents, siblings or partner because you have different agendas and values to them. For instance, if you want to study poetry but your father wants you to work in a bank, you are going to clash over which direction to proceed. In the sentence above, replace 'your father' with 'your conscious mind' and 'you' with 'your subconscious' and you can see how the relationship between your 'inner adult' (conscious) and your 'inner child' (subconscious) works.

Happy 'couples' have learnt to understand and accept the other person's differences and work with them, rather than judge and blame their partner for not being the same as them. These couples have developed a sense of mutual respect towards each other's differences. They expect some sort of natural friction or disagreements to occur in their relationship because they fundamentally understand that the other person is not an extension of their thoughts and feelings, but has the right to their own preferences and values. They argue but they quickly fall back on ways to resolve these natural arguments.

Similarly, happy people are happy because they have a good working relationship *within* themselves. Happy people fundamentally like themselves, even if they act in seemingly contradictory ways, such as being charitable one day and very hard-nosed and pushy the next. They have learnt to accept themselves as a whole and might even celebrate their inner diversity.

Conversely, without exception every client that I have seen in my consulting rooms has seen me because of some sort of conflict with their inner self, some form of a falling out with another aspect of themselves that they do not know how to resolve.

In a therapy session with couples or parent–child conflicts, I make it clear that there are two sides involved in this relationship and that it is the *quality* of the relationship that causes problems between them and needs to improve and I'd say exactly the same thing to you about your mind. The quality of your relationship with your subconscious mind will determine your overall emotional health and happiness. Improving the quality of this relationship is one place where you can consciously exert enormous leverage and influence over your subconscious mind. You may not be able to consciously control a trauma or phobia or some other irrational feeling, but you certainly do have conscious power over the *way* you treat your subconscious mind – what you say and, more importantly, *how* you say it.

There's a right way and a wrong way to approach every single person on this planet and gain their cooperation. In other words, some buttons will rub a person completely the wrong way, while others can make them melt and make you seem like an angel. The right way to get in my wife's good graces is plenty of neck massages, giving her compliments and taking an active interest in her day (all generally highly recommended). The wrong way is not being present, not paying attention, being demanding, complaining or criticising. In short: kindness, empathy and consideration for the needs of others go a long way. As the saying goes, you catch more flies with honey than with vinegar.

Needless to say, there's a right way and wrong way to try to change your subconscious mind. Simply demanding your subconscious changes according to your needs and agenda, without any regard for *its* needs (while throwing in blame, criticism and judgement to boot), is the least effective way to get it to change. Paying attention and respecting its agenda and needs, giving it the odd meta-phorical neck massage from time to time, gets you a lot further.

If that seems so simple, then why is it that I witness all sorts of otherwise highly intelligent people continuing to berate, belittle, blame, demean and criticise their subconscious mind for its behaviour when these same people would never treat other human beings that way? If I treated my wife, or any other person dear to me, as if they were my slave, shouting at them and criticising them, pretty soon I would no longer have that person around in my life. Is it any wonder that our subconscious mind resents when this type of behaviour is directed towards it?

So why is it that we treat such an important part of ourselves so harshly?

The simple conclusion must be that we do not understand the nature of the subconscious mind – this invisible entity we share the same abode with.

Imagine if you shared a house with someone you never saw and who could only speak a few hazy words that you could understand (like 'hunger' or 'tired' or 'bored'). You wouldn't know how to talk appropriately at this person's level because you wouldn't even know if you were talking to an adult or a young child. You would need to spend time getting to understand this person so you could communicate with him/her and get along better.

Similarly, if you got to understand the nature of your subconscious mind, in turn it would help you to understand how to 'talk' with it, how to ask it for things and how to lead it to consider other more helpful points of view.

Understanding your subconscious mind

In our ignorance of our subconscious mind, we keep drawing the wrong conclusions. From these wrong conclusions we form an unhelpful and critical attitude that damages our relationship with it. We end up creating a hostile work environment for our subconscious mind and our poor subconscious mind either gets performance anxiety (and messes results up even more) or gets in a huff with our conscious mind and refuses to listen to our demands any more. There are certain aspects of our subconscious mind's nature that we would greatly benefit from understanding and which would end up vastly improving our relationship with it.

Different nature

Brain scans have shown that women tend to use more areas of their brain simultaneously, while men tend to use more localised areas. Each system has its relative advantages and disadvantages. Women can multi-task better than men but can be overwhelmed by too many things that clamour for attention. Men are more single-focused, which means they can hang onto a problem longer, but they can become so fixated on a problem that they don't know when to let go.

In other words, men and women often use different parts of their brains to solve the same issues. It's not the different methods that are the problem, since both lead to the same results. The problem is when some men or women refuse to acknowledge the relative pros and cons of the other sex's brain, leading to a war of the sexes.

Your conscious and subconscious minds are also very different and any negative focus on the differences can lead to a war of the two minds.

We have to accept that our subconscious mind is the polar opposite of our conscious mind. The yin to our yang. Here are some basic differences between them so you can appreciate the contrast.

The Conscious Mind...	The Subconscious Mind...
is about *doing*	is about *being*
is a time-keeper, keeping its eye on the endless 'to do' list	wants to enjoy and spend time on something that feels good in the now
feels the need to strive and do and achieve	likes to play, be stimulated and entertained
aims to be disciplined and responsible and prepare for the future	can get absorbed in the here and now and forget all about the future
is all about thought and tackles a problem with formal logic and reason	is all about feelings and uses intuition and creativity
tends to consider the subconscious mind as immature, irresponsible, disorganised, undisciplined and fickle	sees the conscious mind as overly serious, overly responsible, boring and unimaginative

Is one mind 'better' than the other?

There is no 'better' or 'worse' answer possible. It depends on your goals and the kind of balance you currently have in your life.

Sometimes it's appropriate to engage the focus and 'doing' capabilities of the conscious mind; sometimes it's healthier to stop working so hard, relax and take a moment to smell the proverbial roses. Sometimes logic can really limit us and switching to imagination and creativity allows us to think outside the box. The conscious has to learn to respect (even enjoy) these differences, rather than judge them on its own terms.

The main players of your subconscious mind

The subconscious mind is a real paradox – it is simple and straightforward in some ways, mind-bogglingly complex in others. I'll try to keep it simple and focus on just two aspects of the subconscious mind that I employ time and time again in therapy to achieve results across the majority of health problems I come across and which will form the main focus of self-help therapy in this book.

These two aspects are in the form of metaphors. The first one is thinking of the subconscious mind as a child.

The second metaphor is much more general and simply refers to working with 'parts' of your subconscious mind. For example, if you had a phobia, you would look to work with the 'protective part' of your mind or if you had an addiction you would look at the 'stimulation-seeking' part of your mind.

Using these two models of the subconscious mind, I've successfully treated depression, anxiety, OCD, self-esteem issues, relationship problems and other conditions with clients who have already tried other conventional psychiatric and psychological methods to no avail.

In general, whenever I want to work on self-esteem, self-confidence, motivation, depression, worry and insecurity I work with using with the first metaphor – of the subconscious mind as a child. Whenever I work with specific fears, traumas and unwanted behaviours, I use the second metaphor. It is possible for there to be an overlap of approaches, so this is a guideline more than a rule and if you feel it's more appropriate for you to work with one approach more than other, then please feel free to do so. However, I do advise reading the material on both as you may learn a good deal about your subconscious mind that can help you on your journey.

Subconscious mind as child

You may already have come across the term 'inner child'. Many people instantly smirk or groan when they hear this term as it evokes images of touchy-feely and overly sentimental and indulgent therapy. In fact, I used to be cynical myself before my experiences in this area, but after years of working in the field, my advice is 'don't throw the baby out with bathwater!' Previous poor application of an idea does not mean the idea itself is poor. Ultimately, what matters are results and this method continues to get fantastic results for my clients, so I'd advise you to put aside any doubts and try using this technique for yourself before you make a judgement.

Is there really an inner child? I've heard some therapists facetiously proclaim that they've checked the X-rays and there is no inner child to be found. Of course, this rather misses the point, as at the neuro-biological level, the 'aim of all psychotherapy is to alter connections in the brain so that real or imagined stimuli no longer evoke the same response'.[2] In other words, metaphors can create 'real' changes in our brains and in our realities and one such very effective metaphor is that of the inner child.

Exercise for getting to know your inner child

So as a starting point, so you can get an experience of this metaphor for yourself, here is a quick exercise:

1. Stand (or at least sit) on one side of the room. From this position I'd like you to 'identify' just with your conscious mind – i.e. notice your perspective from your conscious mind's point of view. As I have already noted above, the conscious mind is synonymous with 'left-brained' thought and logic.
2. Then scan your body and tune into where you feel your 'emotional' self to mostly inhabit. When you've located where you feel your emotional self most resides, imagine your emotional self floating out from inside you to stand two metres away, facing you across the room.
3. Now observe and describe your emotional self. What does he or she look like and what age best describes him or her?

---

2 Bear, Connors and Paradiso: Neuroscience: Exploring the Brain (2000 – 2nd Edition)

In my experience, after thousands of sessions of asking my clients to do this, everyone has, without exception, perceived their emotional self to be in the form of a child, even people who've never come across the inner-child idea before.

4. Now consider how you would describe your *relationship* towards your emotional self and how your logical, conscious self feels about it. After getting past the initial 'feels a bit weird or silly' phase, allow yourself to begin to tune in and express your relationship with your emotional self in terms of frustration, exasperation and anger ('why can't he just do "X"' or 'why won't he just listen to me?'), resentment ('she's always intruding and annoying me' or 'I've tried everything...why can't he just stop nagging me and let me sleep?'); confusion ('I just don't know what he wants from me'); contempt ('she's so weak and pathetic') or guilt ('I feel like a bad person for ignoring and not looking after her').

Now let me ask you a question. If you were to see an adult talking to a real child this way, what would your impression of that adult be as a parent? You might well conclude they were: uninterested and lacking in empathy; impatient, abrupt and brusque; critical and blaming; or simply too wrapped up in their own issues to comprehend the needs of someone else. That's exactly the kind of relationship we have tended to fall into with regards to our emotional selves and it's a very dysfunctional one.

You might have seen the TV series *Supernanny*, where an experienced nanny goes to rescue beleaguered parents from their tearaway children who are running rampant in the house. The story is always the same: the parents start off being stressed, exhausted, short-sighted, confused, impatient and at their wits' end regarding their children. Their 'management' style has usually been either overly disciplinarian and controlling, or overly lax, ineffective and indecisive. The nanny focuses on *teaching the parents* how to be better managers of their children and then it seems everything falls into place. She rarely blames the children themselves for their behaviour, but sees it as a function of the parents' management style.

I see a lot of parallels with those parents on *Supernanny* with how my clients act towards their own emotional selves in my sessions. Needless to say, therapy is also along the same lines as the *Supernanny* programme and just as effective. As I assist my client to become a better manager of their own relationship towards their inner self, there's often a massive positive global effect. One thing I see a lot with clients is that by improving their relationship with their subconscious mind, they access more of the positive qualities of the subconscious mind, becoming less serious and more playful, spontaneous and creative. And their partners comment that they're a lot more fun to be around.

What is the 'mental age' of the inner child?

If we all have the equivalent of an inner child inside of us, perhaps the first question should be what's his/her mental age?

After all, there's a big difference between an inner child who might be four years old and one who might be ten.

Have you ever had the experience of looking at your reflection when there are two mirrors, one in front and the other to the side? The effect is a reflection within a reflection, so you see yourself looking at yourself all the way into infinity. Now imagine you can step out and observe all those versions of yourself, but this time starting right from your birth all the way until the present, each reflection a day older than the last. All these versions of you exist all together at once. Of these multitudes of inner children contained inside, some will tend to be more prominent than others. What often determines the prominence of some ages over others is the amount of 'trauma' experienced at impressionable and formative times of our lives, which leads to a form of 'arrested development'. So if I experience a trauma at the age of eight, some of my emotional development will have become stuck at age eight. From then on, that inner eight-year-old aspect of me will keep rearing its head and 'acting its age' through me until those traumas get unstuck and resolved. When that happens, it can take its place among the other multitudes and move on.

Case study: David's inner child rivalry

One of my patients, David, was in his thirties, married with children. When he came to see me he told me that everything was going well for him until he reported experiencing a personality change. He would become uncharacteristically needy, tearful, sentimental and demanding from his wife.

What transpired was that David had experienced an interrupted childhood when he was 11 years old, when his father left his mother. The mother herself had not developed much of her adult side and needed looking after, so she expected her son to fill the vacuum caused by her husband's absence and take over the mantle of 'man of the house'. The mother needed someone to confide in, support her, help her write letters and organise paying bills and so on. In effect, the young David had to put aside his boyhood and rush to manhood. The inner child therefore remained stuck at 11 years old, biding its time until it could pick up from where it left off. When David's children reached the age he had been when his father had left his family, it had had enough of waiting in the wings and felt it was time it was owed its dues. It saw the attention David's children was getting from both parents and wanted David's conscious mind to start parenting it again. However, David's conscious mind already had its hands full looking after David's two real-life children and so continued to neglect the inner child. That was the source of the tears and feeling unloved.

Therapy involved leading David to acknowledge his unmet needs and then teaching him to re-parent that part of him until its needs were met. As he travelled through that process, David could once again access the other sides of him again as a loving husband and father.

Perhaps you've had experiences in your own life where you've felt the input of your parents was interrupted or incomplete in some way, leading you to feel as if you were stuck in those areas? Let me assure you that it is possible to move past those blocks and to pick up from where things were left off.

It's possible for more than one inner child to be prominent at any time. In the same way that round your family table you might have a little child talking and next to them an older angry teenager also talking, sometimes subconsciously we have the equivalent dynamic in play.

The personality of your inner child

When you are in touch with your inner child side (and providing your inner child has not been sidetracked by other unresolved concerns), then you are probably at your most spontaneous, creative, fun, charming and charismatic. If you find you can tap into this side of yourself quite quickly and easily, then you've at one time or another probably heard other people tell you that you have a certain 'boyish' or 'girlish' charm. However, there is more to the inner child side than just being fun and playful like a child.

At times your inner child can swing between from secure to needy; or from agreeable and cooperative to defiant and rebellious; or from playful to moody and morose, as well as many other points on the continuum of behaviour. I see these contrasting behaviours in my own children. Sometimes my kids are very engaging; other times they signal 'back off give me my own space'. Sometimes they are very cooperative and sometimes they feel the need to push their boundaries to see how far they can go. As long as there is movement and flow across the continuum of behaviours, then I think that's quite natural. However, if you find that your inner child is mostly 'needy' or 'insecure' or 'defensive' then it might well have become 'stuck' on one aspect of its personality and consequently failed to connect with the other ones that would make it more rounded and whole.

In my experience, people I see who describe themselves as neurotic, anxious, sad, demotivated, tearful, confused, unassertive or angry tend to have an unhappy inner child. There are two main reasons that an inner child can be unhappy. The first is that the inner child has indeed experienced some form of 'arrested development' in their past and got stuck at that unresolved phase of their development. In this case the inner child needs to be 'de-traumatised' from this event that led them to being stuck.

The second is that the inner child's emotional needs have been consistently ignored by their inner adult and the inner child feels that their inner adult is unwilling or unable to do anything about it, so they despair about the situation improving in any way in the future – which is a pretty depressing thought for the inner child to have. If sadness dominates its life, then that will block it from tapping into its natural fun-loving side.

Carrot-and-stick feedback

Decisions you make on behalf of your inner child's needs might be a 'hit-or-miss' affair. Your inner child will seek to guide your decisions using a very simple principle – it will reward you with feeling good when you undertake action that makes it thrive and prosper and it will punish you with bad feelings if it feels you took the wrong decision that could sabotage or prevent it from flourishing. In short, it's giving you feedback using a 'carrot-and-stick' approach.

If you look at the behaviour of a really small child, you'll notice that when they are tired, bored, hungry or feel neglected, they will whinge or cry to get their parents' attention. The message is: 'Do I look happy to you? Make things better for me!' Once the parents have listened to the needs of their child and done something about them, the child's gratitude (in whatever form it takes – hugs, kisses, happy cooing) will usually make the parent feel all gooey and warm inside and thus act as a 'reward' for pleasing the child.

That's pretty much what the inner child does with our conscious mind. It communicates with us by sending distress calls and then giving us a feeling of well-being and contentment when we have addressed the distress call. Some of these distress calls are easier to interpret than others.

When my own children were very young and before they could talk, we quickly learnt when they were crying because they were hungry or thirsty, but it was less clear to us when they were crying because they wanted to let us know that were bored, over-tired or had some kind of tummy upset. Some signals were easier to understand than others and it took a while and patient observation to understand what our children were trying to communicate to us.

Now apply this same principle to the needs of your own inner child. Sure, you're probably pretty good by now at understanding his or her physical needs (hunger, thirst, cold, tiredness), but how good are you at interpreting your child's emotional, mental or even spiritual needs? For instance, if your inner child is bored, you will have the experience of a feeling fed up of the current situation and an accompanying strong desire to change it. You may understand your child's underlying message – 'bored now – entertain me' – but do you know what kinds of stimulation it needs? Do you know if it is looking for physical stimulation (exercise or a walk in the park?); emotional stimulation (needing company or socialising with friends); mental stimulation (reading a book or doing a crossword?); even spiritual stimulation (is it looking for a sense of belonging and connectedness to something greater that itself?).

It's not always easy to match the specific unmet need with the appropriate solution. But help is at hand – in later chapters I will instruct you how to get good at identifying and satisfying your inner child's needs.

The inner adult

If the inner child represents your subconscious mind and your more emotional side, then your conscious mind represents your more 'adult' self and your logical and analytical side. The inner child has a set of physical, emotional and mental needs that need looking after and it is your inner adult that is in charge of discerning and meeting these needs.

When the inner adult is rested and not distracted by other concerns, the inner adult side of you can be an excellent problem solver and can approach challenges in a mature and responsible way. Unfortunately, the inner adult is beset by constant demands, leading it to become stressed, anxious, exhausted, beleaguered, short-sighted, confused, guilty, critical, withdrawn, overly disciplinarian or controlling or overly lax and ineffective or indecisive. In addition, some people who identify mostly with their conscious mind can seem very serious, overly responsible and unimaginative, often expressing a dogmatic drive for efficiency at the expense of relationships. Such individuals are often also considered rather boring, because during conversations they tend to overload the listener with detail and facts and express little emotional connection to the topic at hand.

It is better to be more in touch with the inner child or with the inner adult? There is no better or worse side. Each side has its pros and cons and both are needed for a healthy psyche. The aim is to be in touch with both sides of our selves and to have the flexibility to switch between both sides of our personality as and when needed.

If your inner child can at times be subdivided into the playful child, the engaging child, the defiant child, the needy child and the like, the inner adult can similarly be subdivided into different aspects: the parent, the manager, the diplomat, caveman, the policeman/woman and the philosopher, to name but a few.

The parent and manager parts are similar in that they represent the part of us that is in charge of looking after our households as well our businesses (a manager is often like a parent to their business) – both in terms of emotional management as well as the more logistic and practicalities side (making shopping lists, doctor's appointments etc.). The diplomat is in charge of seeking a civilised, diplomatic solution; the caveman represents the part of us interested in a more aggressive, uncivilised, undiplomatic solution; the policeman/woman looks after rules and conduct; and the philosopher represents a calmer, more objective and neutral part of your conscious mind that can act as the voice of sanity and reason when you feel you are losing it. It's like your wiser inner grandparent calming down your stressed inner adult, reminding him or her to take a few deep breaths and focus back on the bigger picture or perhaps to remind you that that your conduct is straying from your values.

I won't go into too much detail in this area, but I want you to be aware that there are other aspects of your personality that you can call upon when needed. For instance, one lady I worked with came to see me because she felt she did not know how to be appropriately assertive with people in certain contexts. What's interesting about this lady was that she was also an accomplished kick boxer. In short it seemed that in such situations she was calling upon the diplomat to assist her when diplomacy was wasted with the people she was dealing with and occasionally she would call in the kick boxer when diplomacy would have benefited more. Therapy was simply about calling in the kick boxer when butt was needed to be kicked and calling in the diplomat when diplomatic solutions should have been offered first. In Chapter 4, I will explain how you too can learn how to call upon different aspects of your conscious mind that would serve you better.

Working with 'parts' of the subconscious mind

Sometimes your subconscious mind will act in irrational or unusual ways that cannot always be best explained by the inner-child aspect of your personality. Indeed it's almost as if there is a more primitive 'part' of you that is carrying out some sort of objective (ostensibly on your behalf) and in a way that, to your complete dismay, is irrespective of your wishes and quite often unnecessary. For instance, if you eat food that you know is bad for you, it won't necessarily be because your inner child needs comforting. The part responsible for your overeating can compel you to gorge yourself on sugary, high-calorie food regardless. It's as if this part of you thinks 'my orders are to stock up with sugary food in case I need to rely on those reserves in the future'. This instinctive strategy made sense in a time in our past where famine was commonplace and we had to stock-pile reserves, but nowadays we are swamped with access to sugary and high-calorie foods, making this strategy very dangerous to our physical health since it can lead us to keep stockpiling reserves that we never use up.

These parts of our behaviour remind me of the Special Service hovering around the President of the United States. The President has his own agenda, but his Special Service has its own agenda about the President, which takes precedence. When the Special Service deem it 'necessary', they will bundle the President halfway out of a wonderful meal, shove him rudely in the back of a car and drive off, even if the threat was very ambiguous and unclear. That's what your parts are like. They are happy to leave you to your own affairs, but whenever one of their mission objectives presents itself, they will take matters in their own hands and you will be carried along in the wake of their momentum, seemingly powerless to resist.

Parts[3] can variously refer to any other aspect of the subconscious mind which governs our behaviour, but the main ones I will be focusing on will be:

* **protective parts** – protect us from pain and control things like phobias and traumas
* **pleasure-seeking parts** – make us pursue pleasure and so govern addictions or excess indulgence in pleasure
* **engineering parts** – govern physiological processes e.g. pain, tissue repair, sleeping etc. and so can be responsible for psychosomatic pain and problems.

Protective – or soldier – parts

Protective parts are like loyal and very diligent, but slightly dim, bodyguards or soldiers that your subconscious has created to protect you from potential threats. These parts are fanatical about their orders and can't see the wood for the trees. That's why if I tell them to 'protect me from spiders', they have no sense of proportion or context and

---

3 In NLP, the term 'parts' is a metaphorical way of talking about the fact that the system of beliefs, states, ideas and abilities which make up an individual's consciousness is composed of various sub-systems that can operate more or less independently of one another. The concept of 'parts' was first described by John Grinder and Richard Bandler in their book *The Structure of Magic Volume 2* (1976)

will insist on protecting me from even the small harmless garden variety of spider in the same heavy-handed manner as for a really dangerous poisonous spider – and regardless of all my rational protestations in the process ('there's no need to be scared, this garden spider can't hurt me').

A parallel with the rigid thinking of soldier parts can be drawn in modern life with the notorious workings of the health and safety (H&S) board. In Britain and the US, most people feel the H&S boards have run amok and lost their way. As writer Pat Williams has commented,[4] H&S was introduced in the first place because of injuries that sprang from callousness and carelessness, mainly in the workplace. However, in the zeal to spot and establish H&S, lines of common sense have been continuously crossed. For instance, take the closure of Scottish bothies, or public unlocked huts, which provide basic shelter in remote mountainous areas for walkers and mountain climbers. They were closed because they were 'unsafe' as they had an entrance but no alternative exit. In other words: safe refuge was denied in the interests of 'safety'. Williams goes on to add, 'This rigidity is, of course, the mark of closed minds and bureaucratic thinking – rules set in stone, applied without discrimination, with no sense of, or even *interest* in, when the line between usefulness and obstruction has been crossed.'

Protective parts are not just concerned with protection from physical threats, but also perceived threats to status and ensuring emotional needs are being met. For instance, giving and receiving attention is a fundamental emotional

---

4 The Pat Williams Page – *Human Givens Journal* Vol 18, No.2 – 2011

human need. Babies and children crave constant attention from parents because attention is associated with care and love. As a young child, if you feel you've got love and care, you can then rest assured that you will survive and thrive because parents who respond with love and care are more likely to look after you rather than reject and abandon you. So attention-seeking is used by babies and young children as a form of checking their survival gauge or abandonment barometer. This seems odd to us parents because we do so much for them and at other times our children will even tell us that they know we love them more than anything and would do anything for them. But when those protective parts of theirs are dominant, all the endless displays of love and affection we've already given them count for nothing. The context is overlooked in the dogged, single-minded pursuit of securing 'enough' attention. This insecurity is even more evident once a second child enters the scene. The older child will feel threatened and compete for attention as if love were a commodity we could only bestow upon either one child or another.

Pleasure-seeking parts

Pleasure-seeking parts are like little indulgent grandmothers offering you sweet after sweet on your birthday because they love the look of pleasure on your face. In my case, my own Greek grandmother would fuss over me at mealtimes to make sure I was officially stuffed. If 2,500 calories of food would make me grow big and strong, then my grandmother would aim to make me eat 4,000-plus calories *just in case* – so there was no shadow of a doubt that my body lacked this important substance. Again, in her desire to ensure I 'survive' and not die of starvation, my grandmother would lose all sense of moderation and perspective (and if anything put me off my food and want to make me rush to leave the table).

Pleasure-seeking parts drive us to partake and over-indulge in something that *feels* good to us (e.g.: smoking, drug use, gambling, pornography) and to 'stock up' or hoard things – eating and drinking to excess or buying stuff we don't need or would never use.

Even though these parts seem to be 'pleasure-seeking', I don't believe they are always driven by pleasure per se, but are driven by a fear of not surviving. After all, survival is not just about avoiding pain and what can harm you but also pursuing what can *enhance* your survival – namely, food and sex (not spreading our genes can be likened to a survival threat).

Engineering parts

I think of engineering parts as brilliant technicians, who are fantastic at directly running the body's mechanisms, but who slightly lack common sense in other areas. In hypnosis one can variously negotiate with the relevant engineering part to do quite a lot of cool things: tone down pain (even induce anaesthesia), rebalance sleep, defuse an allergy, reduce tinnitus, alleviate headaches and even improve eyesight (by easing up the pressure on the capillaries supplying the liquid in the eyes or tightening up the muscles around the lens of the eye itself to bend the lens back into shape).

The seeming flaw with engineering parts is that they can create a new and often worse kind of engineering problem in order to rectify a previous one. For instance, if I've let my stress levels rise unchecked, I sometimes get a tension headache. That's a signal from the engineers to let me know I've been overdoing it and I need to ease up on what is stressing me. It hasn't occurred to them that the last thing I need when I'm stressed is a headache on top of my other stress, as it just gets me more stressed. Unexplained chronic pains, such as neck or back pains, can also be examples of engineering parts trying to make a point about something they want us to pay attention to, with the pain becoming so deafening that it drowns out the underlying message the engineers wanted to convey.

Understanding your parts

While most people can get a sense or sharing their body with a younger, child-like version of their selves, they have difficulty in accepting that they also share it with a team of what variously looks like overzealous soldiers, brilliant if slightly autistic engineers and hedonistic pleasure-seekers who look like they took their inspiration from a combination of George Best, Oliver Reed and Anna Nicole-Smith.

All parts can seem like mindless automatons hell bent in the pursuit of their goals and simply do not know when enough is enough – whether they're creating panic at the sight of a small harmless insect (protective parts); creating psychosomatic pain to meet some other need, such as attention (engineering parts); or overindulging in substances we know we will regret (pleasure-seeking parts). Parts need to be shown how their actions in the present are causing bigger problems in the future. In fact, because the simple function of parts is to 'mindlessly' pursue a goal, they behave to all intents and purposes in an amoral way. For instance, if a part is ordered to 'get attention', it doesn't stop to debate whether the attention it pursues is positive or negative. Attention is attention, as far as parts are concerned. So as children we might end up doing naughty behaviour to gain attention, much to the exasperation of our parents, who are already up to their necks in other demands. As teenagers, 'naughty' behaviour can include criminal behaviour, because that still gets attention – if nothing else, at least among one's peer group. Remember that if protective parts act like soldiers, then these soldiers only exist to serve *our* interests and can be very ruthless in their pursuit of them. For instance, they are completely unconcerned about causing any collateral damage that may be caused to others in the process. They just don't see that as their problem. The only way to modify their behaviour so that they don't intentionally hurt others with their behaviour is to sell them the idea that it would also be in *my* best interests to maintain good relationships with those around us who we value, otherwise I might suffer too. Otherwise they couldn't care less about what's in the interests of others.

Understanding the nature of parts, though, helps to explain a lot of our contradictory behaviour that is otherwise baffling. For instance, it might come as a big surprise to people who want to be free of smoking, drinking, gambling, excessive worrying, having irrational fears or psychosomatic pain to learn that those parts of our subconscious mind running those behaviours and symptoms have been insisting on continuing those unwanted behaviours because they are *convinced* they are actually *helping* us.

If we bear in mind that everything happens for a reason, regardless of how seemingly irrational and contradictory things seem on the surface, that will help us to stop jumping to conclusions that our subconscious minds are having some sort of sadistic fun at our expense. There is always motive behind their seeming madness.

For instance, what could possibly be helpful about keeping someone smoking? Aren't the dangers of smoking well known to everyone nowadays? In fact, the part running smoking behaviour strongly believes that cigarettes fulfil a number of important benefits for its 'host'. First off, people tend to start smoking as teenagers in order to fit in, to look more grown up. As adults we might smoke to socialise or to relax or because we are bored or fidgety and we want something to occupy our minds. Many women smoke because they believe smoking helps cut down their appetite, so that they remain slim and more attractive.

These emotional needs – fitting in, being the most attractive we can be, having stimulation (or at least staving off boredom); relaxing and having a little ritual are all valid healthy human needs. Your subconscious mind *should* be pursuing such unmet needs on your behalf or it would be negligent and derelict in its duty. We don't have a problem with *what* those parts have been trying to do, just the *way* they have been trying to achieve those needs. Unfortunately, the parts have ended up creating far more serious problems than the ones they've originally tried to solve.

That being the case, what prevents parts listening to our endless protests about their methods and then updating their behaviour accordingly? Intellectually we know that becoming a prisoner inside one's house for fear of seeing a spider causes far more pain than if we were even bitten by a common spider. So why can't parts see that and do something about it? The simple answer to this is that it is simply not in their nature to operate that way. Logically, our conscious minds can easily spot the more serious fall-out caused by the methods parts choose. However, parts do not have formal logic. They use a kind of 'emotional logic'. A classic protective parts response to something like spiders usually goes as follows:

- Step 1: (due to some early emotionally charged experience), the part thinks: 'I've been told that our number one threat is spiders.'
- Step 2: 'Therefore, my job is to avoid spiders at all costs. If I avoid all possible contact with spiders, then I'll be safe. In order to avoid spiders I need to stoke up the fear centres. The more fear there is, the more vigilant my "host" will be, so I need to max out on the fear so that not a single spider will escape our notice.'
- Step 3: 'Once I'm safe from spiders, I can finally relax and not have to worry about them. I'll be free.'
- Step 4: 'Now that I'm free of the possibility of contact with spiders, I can get on and do the thing I want to do.'
- Step 5: 'If I get on to do the things I want to do, I'll have fulfilled my potential and be satisfied and happy.'

The snag with this type of 'reasoning' is that the part always ends up simply getting their 'host' stuck on the initial stage of fear, which means they never get to progress and experience the good stuff – the benefits further up the ladder (like achieving fulfilment and happiness). As part of its conditions for moving up the ladder, the part has insisted on a cast-iron guarantee ('to know there are absolutely no spiders near me'). Because there are no guarantees in this universe (except death and, unfortunately, taxes), then the part will never get its assurances met so that it can move on up. It can always argue 'What if one spider slipped through unnoticed, onto my clothes or my hair?' It has become stuck in a trap of its own making.

Exercise for getting to know your parts

In the same way described earlier in the exercise for getting to know your inner child on pages 21–22, you can similarly get to know any part of you which is causing you some conflict or concern, so you can begin to understand it and then in due course, be in a position to lead it to adopt a new behaviour.

1. Firstly, find a nice comfortable spot to sit in, then scan your body and tune into where you feel this part of you most acts out from – your heart or stomach, perhaps. When you've located where you feel this part of you most resides, imagine this part floating out of that location to stand onto the palm of one of your hands.
2. Notice and describe this part. Note that, unlike doing this exercise with the inner child, parts may appear in non-human representations. Sometimes they appear as balls, blobs, clouds or geometric shapes. Just notice any other sensations you are experiencing with this part: texture

(e.g.: smooth, tingly or prickly); movement (e.g.: spinning); temperature (warm, hot, cold); weight (light, heavy or weightless).

3. Now describe your *relationship* towards this part of you. If you've picked a phobic part, perhaps you experience a sense of infuriation and exasperation, summed up by words such as 'You know these little spiders can't hurt you so why can't you just stop being so silly and afraid?' or 'What's wrong with you?' If you've picked up smoking or the substance abuse part, perhaps you find yourself saying something to that part along the lines of 'You know smoking is bad so why can't you just stop like Bob did?'

4. Then imagine how that part of you might respond in turn from its perspective, as if it had a little microphone or as if you were to add thought bubbles to it, just like you see in characters in a cartoon.

Hopefully you'll have a sense from that part that it's not just causing you problems for the sake of it, but it's got something else in mind. We'll pick up on this technique later on but for now I'd like you to know that when you get to know parts better, understand where they're coming from and see things from their perspective, you'll soon understand their reasons and how you end up creating your own roadblocks to change.

When change fails to happen, many people can be quite harsh on themselves and think that deep down they don't really want to change. This is only partly true. The conscious mind could well be absolutely committed to change (otherwise people who see therapists wouldn't be willing to make big sacrifices in their time and money to see them), but it does not know *how* to collaborate with these parts of the subconscious mind to get them on its side, so an impasse is created between the conscious and the subconscious mind.

The forthcoming chapters will show you how to communicate with your subconscious mind in a way it can really comprehend and lead to change.

Conclusion

In my experience, the vast majority of emotional and psychological problems, as well as all psychosomatic problems, can be explained, one way or another, through one or both of these two metaphors of the subconscious mind – parts and the inner child.

In the next chapter I'll provide some general tips on how to make your subconscious mind do what you want it to. These work for both the inner child and parts. In the chapters after that I'll talk in more detail about what is specifically required for working with each aspect and will go into more detail with how the problems created by parts and the inner-child aspects of the subconscious mind can explain conditions such as depression, OCD, addictions and even many relationship problems.

2
How to Get Along With Your Subconscious Mind

'Seek first to understand, then be understood.'

– Mahatma Ghandi

IT'S IMPORTANT TO REALISE THAT IF YOU DON'T UNDERSTAND the motives of the subconscious, whether it's the protective intention of parts (trying to help you but getting stuck on the way) or the feedback distress signals used by your inner child, then you're liable to misjudge them and unfairly adopt a harsh and unjustified attitude towards them. This in turn will severely damage the quality of your relationship with your subconscious mind.

Let's take a look at unfair attitudes. Jim is on holiday abroad and has booked a ticket for a show at the local circus. There is only half an hour until the performance begins and he's terribly lost. He comes across a local boy, who could help him, but the boy can't speak any English and Jim only knows a few words of his language.

Jim tries to ask for help in English, but the young child looks confused and points him to the police station, which is what he thinks Jim is asking for. Jim begins to get impatient because the boy just doesn't understand him and the show is about to start. Jim repeats his request, this time louder and with an increasing edge to his voice. The child gets a little bit nervous and continues to point Jim to the police station. Jim rolls his eyes, his question begins to turn more into a demand and he even adds an insult on the end: 'I said: where's the c-i-r-c-u-s, thicko.' By this point, the child becomes increasingly nervous of being shouted at by Jim and just wants to appease him so he'll stop shouting. He gestures more emphatically to the police station. Jim throws his arms up in the air and gives up. He looks around for a while but since there's no one else to ask, he returns to the young boy. Jim approaches him in a tense manner, breathing a sigh of frustration and asks the same question in the same way again, all the while his body language and demeanour is shouting: 'Look, you idiot, I've got more important things to do and I'd rather not deal with you, so just tell me where the damn circus is?' The boy looks offended and hurt and runs away. Jim then complains how unhelpful everyone around here is.

Now, in real life you wouldn't act like Jim in this situation, would you? But this is the way that we often treat our subconscious – as if we can browbeat it into doing what we want, instead of realising that our conscious and subconscious minds are different entities. Rather than expecting it to bend to our will, we need to learn to communicate with our subconscious on its level.

Here's the same situation but this time from a different angle. Jim realises that he needs help from the local boy so he decides to try to speak his language. He quickly rummages through his dictionary to learn all the necessary words because he wants to communicate on the boy's level rather than expect him to understand his (after all, Jim is a visitor in his country). He goes up to the boy in a polite manner, grateful and appreciative that this boy is willing to help. The boy can't quite understand Jim's pronunciation of circus and looks blank but instead of blaming him, Jim takes responsibility for his failure to communicate. He tries something new. He starts miming someone riding a horse, then someone juggling and falling down like a clown. Realisation dawns on the boy's face and he breaks into a grin. He knows exactly what Jim is asking. He is only too happy to point him in the right direction. Jim gets to go to the circus.

In short, the keys to getting the results wanted here were: changing one's *attitude*; developing *rapport*; extending *curiosity* towards differences; *respect* and *befriending* rather than fighting. Applying these keys to any of your relationships will immeasurably enhance them. And if you try it with your subconscious, the benefits to you will be astounding.

Upgrading your attitude

The first reason that may prevent you from building rapport and cooperation with your subconscious mind is your general attitude towards your relationship with it. As mentioned in the previous chapter, there's a right way and a wrong way to go about addressing problems in your relationships.

The wrong way is expecting or demanding things go according to your terms and conditions and reacting to any natural misunderstanding and miscommunication as if it were a deliberate attempt to confound and infuriate you or to make your life difficult. We keep repeating our demands without any care or responsibility for *how* we say our demands, nor the impact our choice of words might have on others. We then blame others when their cooperation is no longer forthcoming.

The right way is basically the opposite of all that. If we seek to understand and respect the other person *on their terms*, we tend to stop taking misunderstandings personally and see communication as a joint responsibility. This prevents us going into criticism and blaming mode. The good news is that most people already employ just such a positive attitude towards one or more people in their life. They already know how to do it. It just didn't occur to them to import the skills that work well in one domain into another area of their lives where it would yield similar rewards. So if you're great at dealing with your customers because you smile at them, enquire about their needs and value their custom, try keeping the same 'hat' on with your spouse or partner and see what happens. If you're a stay at home mum or dad who's feeling fed up with your partner, try extending the same leniency and forgiveness towards him or her as you would towards your friends if they were to let you down.

Why attitude affects processing

Your attitude affects your well-being right down to a very basic mechanical level. For instance, I, like most therapists, have many clients who have told me that 'I don't do anger' or 'I refuse to get hurt', as if that's all that's needed to not have the emotion exist in the first place. On the face of it, clamping down on an undesirable feeling or emotion sounds like a sensible thing to do. It doesn't, however, mean that the 'energy' of anger or hurt goes away though. As the Buddhists say, 'What you resist, persists.' All it means is that the energy of the unwanted emotion just gets shifted elsewhere and that unwanted energy invariably ends up seeking a different outlet of expression, such as teeth grinding (for anger) or being very risk-averse (to prevent potential hurt again). You don't have to be a physicist to know that the first law of thermodynamics is 'energy cannot be created or destroyed, but just transformed from one form to another'. So whenever we try to ignore, ban or fight an emotion, we are fighting the very physics upon which the universe operates. Emotions cannot be destroyed; they can only be transformed to another kind of emotion (or, more accurately, they just keep recycling from one emotion into another).

Think the subconscious mind as responsible for placing the feelings and emotions it experiences on a conveyor belt that travels to the conscious mind. The conscious mind is then responsible for validating what is presented to it. All that is needed to validate a feeling or emotion is a simple acknowledgement that it is valid and real – that's it! – and then the feeling or emotion is 'processed' and can move on, allowing room for the next emotion. The conscious mind in effect acts as a rubber stamp to 'authorise' the experience and we gain what's commonly known as 'closure' on the experience.

Validating your subconscious mind

Validation, therefore, is to therapy what 'location, location, location' is to property. Validation is absolutely crucial when it comes to processing feelings and emotions otherwise feelings and emotions get blocked, stuck and then other things start piling on top of those in turn. In fact, it's no exaggeration to say that the majority of the problems people see us therapists for (anger, frustration, resentment, hurt, misunderstanding, relationship conflicts and sadness) are often simply the result of someone's feelings being invalidated – either by someone else or by 'self-invalidation'. By self-invalidation, I mean our conscious mind invalidating our subconscious mind, which is usually expressed as the inner adult invalidating the inner child or one or more parts.

This point is so important that I'd like to state it again: validation means making whatever it is we are feeling feel 'valid' and real to us.

Really it's a way of simply acknowledging our experience or, to put it another way, being given 'permission' to feel what we feel. When you allow yourself to feel what you feel without judgement or qualification, you are in effect 'rubber stamping' that raw feeling with official recognition, which allows it to be processed and integrated with the rest of your feelings.

Validation is not that commonly held mistaken idea that it's just about listening to someone and being sympathetic. It's a bit more than that. As you'll have experienced, invalidation can affect your whole state and mood and ruin your whole day. You will have undoubtedly experienced first hand a time when you've felt compelled to fight for some kind of simple acknowledgement. For instance, an encounter perhaps with a retail shop or a company that made a mistake with your order or service, thoroughly inconveniencing you in the process and then becoming hostile and defensive towards you and refusing to apologise for their role in inconveniencing you. Maybe it's because some staff fear that if they admit they made a mistake, it would lead to liability and lawsuits. In most cases, you, the wronged customer, are not looking for financial compensation, but for a simple admission or acknowledgement that you have been inconvenienced and that you have the right to be upset.

When I worked as a manager of a store and we made a mistake with a customer, in my experience at first all the wronged customer was looking for was a simple apology – a simple admission that through no fault of their own they were inconvenienced – and more importantly that they were *entitled to feel* inconvenienced. However, the more our company denied the customer's experience, the more the customer was left fuming and feeling the need to prove what they felt was real. Ironically, it's only after being badly handled at this first stage that most customers get mad enough to look up a lawyer to try to sue a company. A simple apology that costs nothing would have avoided all of that.

By the same token, if your conscious mind refuses to accept the validity of what your subconscious mind is feeling and experiencing (such as raw anger), in effect the conscious mind is refusing to 'rubber stamp' anger and all associated experiences where anger is present. If your feelings remain invalidated that means they remain unprocessed, blocked, repressed or displaced into somatic complaints or other problem behaviours. That's like creating a pile-up of anger on that metaphorical conveyor belt, which will spill over into other areas, such as physical symptoms, panic attacks, headaches, bad dreams, broken sleep... the list goes on.

It's this second consequence that really causes mental health problems, rather than the original feelings themselves. The fact that you feel anger or hurt or sadness or envy is not itself the problem. These are natural feelings that make you human. It's attempting to deny them and therefore your basic human nature, which ends up becoming the 'real' problem.

Given the importance of validation, why would our conscious mind not want to validate our own emotional experiences?

The simple answer is that our conscious mind has learnt to be very judgemental in its attitude – and judgements and validation don't go together.

Judgements come about from 'judging' things based on upholding some kind of abstract perfect standard (e.g. such as being the perfect, problem-free person or being the perfect parent and always staying calm with the kids). Validation is about accepting things 'as is' and working with them as they are, without any comparisons to perfection. In other words, judgements are about upholding principles, and validation is about being pragmatic and accepting the imperfect context in which things occur.

In our increasingly 'left-brained' world we have learnt to look for solutions by 'analysing' the problem. This analysis though usually takes the form of *'what's wrong; who's to blame; why did they do that in the first place'*. Analysis is a very unforgiving approach that wants to know why things aren't perfect in the first place and then jumps on the people who dared to bring problems into this perfect, unobtainable utopia.

Unlike your conscious mind, as far as your subconscious mind is concerned, there are no good or bad emotions. Every emotion just 'is'. The motto of the subconscious mind is: 'you can only feel what you feel'. If you feel something – no matter how 'inappropriate' – the truth is that you feel it, otherwise you are in a state of denial about your reality.

You can challenge the 'content' associated with feelings, but never challenge the feelings themselves, otherwise you are fighting another person's reality (and they will fight to defend their reality). For instance, if you were expecting a friend to be at your house for dinner by 8 p.m. and they arrive at 9 p.m. without telling you, in the absence of any other information you may have thought that they were being inconsiderate and not respecting your time. If that was the case, then it would be entirely appropriate to be fuming inside and want to give them a piece of your mind when they turn up. However, as soon as they turn up, they start telling you that there was a traffic jam and their mobile phone ran out of battery so they couldn't call you. Your friend asks you to not be angry because it's not their fault. You are still angry, however. As it happens, you became angry over the wrong assumption, but you cannot deny that you are now angry. Someone telling you that you should not be angry may even make you more angry because it invalidates your experience. After all, you are not a machine that can switch your emotions on or off. You need time to let the anger subside naturally, rather than be told not to feel something. It would be better for the late person to say that they regret your understandable anger and if it wasn't for that damn traffic jam, it wouldn't have ruined both your evenings. Even therapists sometimes make this mistake of challenging the feeling rather than the content connected to it.

Case study: Nema's self-judgements

One of my patients, a woman in her late twenties called Nema, came to see me wanting assistance with changing her feelings of frustration and anger. As part of her job in the NHS, Nema had had a lot of training in cognitive behavioural therapy (CBT). CBT teaches a person to rationally challenge their irrational (emotional and subconscious) responses. So during the times that Nema would feel angry and frustrated, she would tell herself, as instructed, 'there's no point in getting upset over something like this' or 'it's no big deal, let it go', but she could not understand why this was not having any effect on her frustration. In our session she came to realise that she had got in the habit of dismissing her feelings by jumping straight to the solutions without acknowledging the validity of her feelings in the first place. She wasn't rubber-stamping them so they could move on. In effect she was implying to her emotional self 'you've no right to feel this way over a trivial matter'. That sounds kind of judgemental to me.

As with our earlier example of the couple, the more a person is ignored and told to 'not feel what they feel', the more those unwanted feelings seek to justify their existence and fight to get heard even more.

Being judgemental is one of the most destructive behaviours we inflict upon ourselves. The widespread judgement that we direct towards ourselves and others is the silent pandemic. It's impossible for us to create any kind of sincere rapport with our subconscious mind if we are privately very critical and judgemental about its nature, because we would be harbouring ill-will and our subconscious mind picks up on this and feels anger, contempt or resentment.

Learning to validate our feelings and experiences (in short, learning to validate our subconscious mind), is a hugely important part of working with both our parts and the inner-child aspects.

Building rapport with your subconscious mind

Once you've improved your attitude towards your subconscious mind, you will be in far better position to build rapport with it and end up in a happier relationship together.

So how do you build rapport with your subconscious? Just look at what you're already doing in some of your closest relationships and notice that you are expressing all those key elements mentioned at the start of this chapter. Then the trick is to make a mental note of applying these keys to yourself.

Let's look at this for a moment, so that you can see how

naturally this can come together once you start off on the right footing.

For the sake of illustration, supposing you were at a party and a friendly neighbour introduced themselves to you. Let's call this friendly person Jack. For Jack to have taken the time to introduce himself to you (and providing he is not covertly networking, trying to recruit you into a multi-level marketing scheme or into a cult!), he must have started out being curious about you and is interested in knowing more about you.

Perhaps during the course of your conversation you share some of the stresses of modern life, how busy you are at work or that you haven't gone out much in the last few years. As you express your feelings, Jack doesn't jump down your throat with solutions in an arrogant 'I know best' manner. Instead he empathises with you and says with genuine sincerity, 'Oh, that must have been a difficult time for you' or 'poor you'.

Now imagine it's a couple of months down the line and you have struck up a close friendship with Jack. During this time Jack has noticed that you have different values in life to his, religious, moral, sporting, literary or whatever and he has accepted and respected those differences without it affecting his sense of friendship towards you.

At another time you phone Jack to tell him that you are going to be late to his barbecue because you are stuck in traffic. Jack responds in a friendly way, trusting your reasons implicitly and appreciating that 'it's the thought that counts'. You are grateful that Jack is so understanding and you mentally vow to make it up to him. The mutual respect is obvious.

Now by way of contrast, let's rewind back in time, give Jack a personality change and remove some of those key elements from his behaviour.

You're back at this party. Jack has seen you around a lot in the background but doesn't seem particularly inclined to want to get to know you. However, for one reason or another, there you are telling Jack about some of things going on in your life and Jack responds by rolling his eyes and then barely seems to listen or pay any real attention at all. He doesn't express any sympathy for your situation.

His eyes keep scanning the room as if he would like to be somewhere else. It's almost as if his body language is saying that he thinks you're a fool and a loser. The implied message is that you shouldn't be annoying him with your problems. You should just sort them out for yourself and stop bothering him and everyone else. Jack either ignores your plight or cuts you off to patronisingly tell you, 'This is what you should do' as though he's the expert of your life and you're a useless twit.

Moreover, Jack thinks your general values and the kinds of things you're into, like art, drawing, poetry, being connected to nature, are just pointless and a waste of time.

On another occasion you turn up late to a BBQ and you apologise to your host because you were stuck in traffic. From the corner of your eye you see that Jack is also present and when he hears you apologising, you catch him rolling his eyes again as if he's thinking 'Of course you're late, because you're an idiot who can't do anything properly'. He never trusts your reasons when things don't go to plan.

One day you hear a banging at your door. You open the door to find Jack explaining that he was on the way to work when his car broke down and he needs your help to get to work. Even while asking you to do something for him, he hasn't taken the usual contempt from his face. Because of the way Jack has asked you and because of the way he has generally treated you in the past, you simply close the door in his face and have no further interest in helping him.

That evening Jack goes to see his therapist and tells him he can't believe how uncooperative you were towards him earlier on. Jack's therapist tells him he shouldn't be surprised given how he's been behaving towards you and that if he wants your cooperation, he should make amends towards you and at the very least Jack should treat you the same way he does his other best friends. Jack agrees and makes a sincere effort to do so. The results could then go in three different ways:

Scenario A: Jack is nice to you but you have been so traumatised in the past when Jack showed you contempt that you simply can't get over the hurt from the way he treated you. You need to be de-traumatised or that trauma of the past will keep interfering.

Scenario B: Jack is nice to you, but you don't trust or believe Jack. You remain wary and suspicious of him. Jack will have to earn your trust over time.

Scenario C: Jack is nice to you, you are nice back and you even lend him your car in the future.

This book is all about leading you towards creating scenario C for yourself, healing the relationship between your conscious and subconscious mind.

Becoming more empathic

Cultivating more *empathy* would have prevented a lot of bad blood happening in the first place with Jack. If Jack were to 'walk a mile in your shoes', so to speak, he would be more understanding and accepting of your world and where you are coming from. The more understanding he was, the less room there would have been for judgements, because judgements are all about having judged you solely on *Jack's* terms, rather than on *your* terms. Judgements are terribly destructive because they stop us learning and they get in the way of open communication.

Even people who show wonderful empathy towards all those around them may still be incredibly unempathetic to themselves (or more accurately, their subconscious mind).

Many people have not thought of being empathetic to themselves because it is quite a novel concept. To treat your subconscious mind with the same respect that you would give another human being is quite a revelation. But once most people grasp this concept, they get on and start being empathetic to themselves.

Other people can't bring themselves to do it because they have become stuck on the old habits of judging, blaming and criticising themselves. They find it incredibly hard to feel empathy and understanding for another part of their personality. I tell such people that empathy is also a choice. Our attitude depends on what we focus on and we have a lot of conscious choice when we choose that focus.

The meta-mirror technique for increasing empathy

There's a simple but powerful technique in NLP called the 'meta-mirror', which is very useful for cultivating more empathy towards another person by creating a virtual experience of what it's like to be in their shoes.

Step 1: Pick someone in your life that you would like to understand better. It could be a family member, partner, friend, colleague or even your boss. Let's call this person Lucy.

Step 2: Imagine Lucy is standing across from you, no more than two metres away. Notice how she appears to you and what are the first things you are aware of as you look at her.

Step 3: Then physically go over and stand in 'Lucy' and be her, as if you were the world's greatest method actor, looking back at yourself. Notice what it's like to be Lucy and how Lucy feels about things.

Many people have used this technique with their clients or customers in order to understand the other person's point of view better. They mention that their customer relationships (and profits) have improved immensely, while some have commented that their personal or romantic relationships have become closer and more respectful. It's a great technique and will form the basis of a lot of inner-child work in a future chapter.

As you increase your levels of empathy towards others, you will find that you become better at validating their feelings because empathy allows you to see things more from the other person's perspective and doing this in turn makes it easier to understand and accept (or validate) the other people's feelings or values around their perspectives.

Getting curious about others and yourself

Curiosity is another quality that acts like engine oil into the overall impact of changing attitude, becoming more empathetic and building greater rapport.

When we are curious, we approach things in a free-spirited, experimental and open-minded way and so we end up learning more. To tune into your natural sense of curiosity, think about the time you first met someone whose ideas fascinated you and got you thinking. You got excited because you started making connections between what this person was saying and other similar experiences in your life and you started integrating all these various snippets of info into some kind of coherent whole and your old perspective started to shift and it felt like you saw the light. And it's exciting! Now consider approaching the whole subject of your subconscious mind in this curious way and as you do, you will find you get more enjoyment from this subject and the whole nature of your subconscious mind becomes even more intriguing.

Building trust with yourself

Trust hasn't been mentioned so far but it is another vital ingredient of a good relationship. If you trust someone, it allows you to have more confidence in their abilities to deliver an outcome or to act in a certain way.

When you trust someone, you don't feel the need to nag, audit or keep tabs on them. Instead you can both use your energy more constructively elsewhere, such as joint projects like renovating the house you both share. If you don't trust them, you end up spending an inordinate amount of time and energy worrying about things they haven't even done – but are anxious they *might* do.

Trust develops naturally from the process of empathy, understanding, respect and building rapport.

Most people who see me have fundamentally mistrusted their subconscious mind on one aspect or another. This in turn has led to an impoverished relationship with their subconscious mind and it expresses itself as insecurity and anxiety in some manner.

One client I recently worked with, Caroline, a 40-year-old woman who had been experiencing anxiety attacks, demonstrated just such a mistrust. Caroline didn't trust her body and always took the view that her anxiety was due to 'crossed wires' or some other biochemical imbalance causing a malfunction. As such, because she felt there was something 'wrong' with her, she worried that she was going to end up mad. It came as a shock to her to learn that her body was functioning 'normally', that it's designed to respond in the way way she was experiencing, in the same way that an alarm clock is designed to give a loud, irritating sound. Just because an alarm clock gives off an unpleasant signal doesn't mean it's not working. If anything it means it *is* working perfectly because it's doing what it's designed to do. Anxiety is simply a message or feedback signal from the subconscious mind that we need to attend to some unmet need. Once the need is met, the 'messenger' of anxiety has done its job and goes away, in the same way that hunger signals go away once you've listened to them and eaten a sandwich. The fact that my client was experiencing anxiety shows that her whole feedback communication system was working. It also shows that she failed to interpret those signals correctly and address the real underlying problem leading to those signals, otherwise those signals would not have persisted for so long.

I believe that our bodies are fundamentally healthy. Our bodies know how to sleep, how to relax and, if you are a man, how to get an erection (many men don't trust their apparatus to work properly). For that matter our bodies also know how to get frightened and run away from something scary.

If our bodies are not sleeping properly or unable to relax or unable to get an erection, it's not always because they are suffering from separate physiological problems. If you put diesel fuel in your non-diesel car, your car would stall. That doesn't mean there is something wrong with your actual car. You wouldn't stop trusting your car and take it to the scrapyard because it's not starting because you gave it the wrong fuel. You know your car could not operate because of an outside interference that has temporarily hijacked the situation. You find a way to siphon out the diesel, put in the correct petrol and then you trust that your car will work again and it will.

Our bodies know how to do all those natural processes as well. If our bodies are not sleeping or relaxing, it's mostly because they've just been temporarily derailed by something that is traumatising it. You fix the trauma and trust that your body will get back on track, and it will.

Befriending rather than fighting

Most of my clients come to my sessions expecting that therapy for their anxiety problem is going to be along the lines of 'getting rid' of that anxiety and 'making it go away', as if anxiety is some sort of infected tonsil that could just be removed.

This is a very misleading viewpoint that leads to inaccurate beliefs about how to fix things. In fact, if you want things resolved, you will need to do the exact opposite of this approach – befriending that anxious part and bringing it back into the fold, as opposed to fighting it. If you befriend it, it's no longer your enemy.

This is such a paradigm shift for most people's thinking that I'd really like to spend a little time laying to rest those old outdated notions about fighting parts of your subconscious mind into submission.

The first point is that trying to 'cut off' a problematic part of your subconscious is always going to be doomed to failure. You couldn't get rid of a problem part even if you wanted to. Think of an anxious part of you as being one of a set of co-joined twins, whose body and physiological processes are so intertwined that they cannot be operated on. The twins are together for life, so they might as well learn to get on and help each other to make the best life possible. For this reason I see the current reliance in a lot of mainstream therapies on distraction techniques to deal with anxiety as limited. If a pair of co-joined twins were bickering and arguing with each other about an ongoing difference of opinion and a therapist relied mainly on distracting them by saying 'Is that a UFO out there?', then it's pretty certain that the twins would simply continue to bicker about their difference of opinion once the distraction wore off.

Secondly, all this approach does is needlessly alienate and exclude that part of your subconscious mind, preventing helpful communication and demolishing rapport. Imagine you have a serious conflict with someone close to you and you both come to see me for some form of 'couples counselling'. By way of illustration, imagine you tell me that your boyfriend and you are both arguing over misunderstandings and miscommunications and your goal for the sessions is 'I just want him to shut up so he stops bothering me. Please can you hypnotise him to shut up?' I would reply to you that in my opinion your relationship problems will not be fixed this way. If you have a couples problem, you have to do couples work and that means working on your relationship and communication.

People often reply, 'Yes, but it's been so hard for so long, I don't care, I just want a result!' Yes it has and you can insist all you like about demanding results up front first and then changing, but it doesn't make good results happen any quicker. The changes happen by changing the mindsets in place first, especially giving up this old cherished notion that all your problems would be solved if you can just make them go away. It doesn't work like that. The conscious mind has to do the necessary work to cultivate a good, healthy relationship and then the changes will occur as a function of that.

Case study: Rebecca and subconscious as enemy

Rebecca came to see me for anorexia and told me about her past experiences in group therapy. The clients were told to view anorexia as 'the voice' and they were encouraged and expected to do everything possible to fight that voice and cut it out. Rebecca got into the habit of fighting that part of her constantly, hour by hour, day after day, year after year, which understandably left her drained and depleted, as well as having no real results after all that time.

She came to see me because she felt she had not fought that voice enough and wanted tips and help to fight it better. I felt Rebecca had given the fighting approach a very good run for its money, so the fact that it hadn't worked suggested to me that the method itself wasn't helpful, rather than that she just hadn't fought hard enough. How much more fighting can one expect that she hadn't already done?

I asked Rebecca to stop seeing the anorexic part as her enemy and look at it from *its* point of view. Rebecca realised that at some point in her past she had been told that being fat is the root of all misery and being slim makes you happy and that part had diligently pursued that idea, even in the face of stiff opposition and criticism from others around it. The part wasn't able to understand why Rebecca was wilfully frustrating its efforts. In order to continue to do its job, which it took very seriously, it was having to divert a lot of its energy to demolishing the barriers Rebecca was putting in its way, leaving everyone feeling exhausted. What eventually created the tipping point in therapy was when Rebecca made peace with that part and gained its cooperation in changing 'fat is the root of all misery' to less extremist goals (of 'being slim and healthy').

Leading people to change

The formula for leading people to change is:

rapport–rapport–rapport–lead

That's three parts of rapport to one part of 'lead'.

Most people who want to change others have a tendency to jump straight to the 'lead' part, overlooking the vital importance of building the necessary rapport first. Good rapport in turn, as discussed throughout this chapter, is a function of putting in place all those keys to change that I've mentioned. Once you have built sufficient rapport with a person (or with your subconscious mind), it's possible to lead them to all sorts of dramatic changes. During my work on the BBC3 series *Freaky Eaters*, it was possible to ask people to participate in all sorts of hair-raising experiences (such as parachuting, wind walking, doing live stand up etc.) because I built good rapport with the people I worked with. They trusted me and they trusted in what I was asking them to do, regardless of how scary it seemed.

This formula works as well with children as with adults. Imagine my daughter Lara tells me, 'Daddy, it's my first day at school and I'm terrified.'

I could ignore what it must feel like to her and jump straight to a solution, such as making light of the situation: 'Don't be silly. You think you've got problems. I've got two mortgages and school fees to worry about, this is nothing.' To which in my mind I imagine my daughter replying with, 'Thanks. I'm still terrified of school and now I also feel ashamed and guilty to boot. Great job of providing the reassurance and understanding I need, Dad!'

Or I could try bringing together all the elements described in this chapter and start with empathising and validating her situation and say something such as: 'Okay, sweetheart, I know you feel terrified and it's easy for me to say "you'll be fine" because I know I survived school, but you don't know how difficult it could be for you.'

As an aside, you may think I'm scaring her when I entertain her unspoken fear and put words to it. In actual fact, the opposite tends to happen. By naming her worst fears I am validating her unspoken feelings associated with those fears. By acknowledging that she has such a fear, Lara would be more likely to think, 'Phew, so I'm not crazy or silly or weak, it's okay for me to feel scared.' Processing has been enabled.

As soon as Lara feels I've understood her, then I've earned her trust and any solutions I mention from this point are going to be more respected by her and better received. So now I can continue with '...but you know my best friends Tom, Dick and Harry, I met them in school and soon you're going to find your own best friends and within a week you'll be having so much fun playing games with them that I'm going to have to drag you out.' Now Lara's attention has been led to a different happy parallel universe where things are nice and she can look forward to pursuing pleasure rather than focusing on avoiding pain.

Rapport–rapport–rapport–lead is a deceptively powerful technique that can be used to lead yourself or others towards desirable outcomes.

The mirror technique to self

Now that you understand the importance of befriending rather than fighting, how might you go about befriending?

Well, you need a system that allows you to assess your relationship with your subconscious mind, build rapport with it and apply the approaches mentioned in this chapter, and also a system that allows you to resolve any conflicts and blocks to a new healthy relationship with yourself.

This system is the 'mirror to self'. It is a variation of the NLP 'meta mirror' described earlier, although in NLP I have only come across it being used with external relationships (conflicts with spouses, family members, colleagues etc), rather than my variation, which is for working with your *internal* relationships.

The mirror to self involves inviting your inner adult (analytical conscious mind), your inner grandparent (calmer, wiser conscious mind) and your inner child (emotional sub-conscious mind) to a family meeting where they can sort out their differences. The stages are as follows:

1. Imagine you are acting as a facilitator or mediator between your inner adult and your inner child. Now imagine a calming place, it could be in a boardroom, living room or outside on a picnic blanket, where you will chair this meeting.

2. In this place, develop a sense of your inner adult floating out of you to stand on one side of you and then, imagine having your inner child float out of you to stand on the opposite site. You yourself are adopting the position of the calmer, wiser inner grandparent.

3. All three aspects of you form three points of a triangle, with you at the apex, like a UN peacekeeper, acting in a neutral capacity, respecting both of these aspects and aiming for a win–win solution.

4. Imagine then floating out of the 'you' in the inner grandparent chairperson position and go into the inner adult, so that you see through its eyes and really access and feel what it feels. Tune into your inner adult, and listen and appreciate its perspective towards the inner child. Get a sense of what its main gripe or bone of contention towards the inner child is and even put this complaint into words addressed directly to the inner child (e.g. 'I despair at you because you never change and you're making my life difficult').

5. Then float out across from the inner adult position and into the inner child and do the same – appreciating this alternative perspective from your subconscious mind and what it feels like to be on the receiving end. In fact,

on this point really allow yourself to notice what it feels like to be judged by the conscious mind across from you, criticising you for just doing your job (or for just acting according to your nature). What would you say back to your inner adult about the way you've been treated and your gripes and complaints about how the inner adult is doing its job? (e.g. 'you don't care about my needs' or 'you never listen' or 'I just need reassurance about...')

6. Having 'walked' in each one's shoes, now float back into your inner grandparent and take stock of both sides of this conflict. Consider, what is it you now know that, armed with this 'insider information', will change the way you see things? What advice can you now offer each part of your mind in turn? For instance, I found myself telling my conscious mind to stop taking life so seriously and being so fixated on outcomes and enjoy the present; and I've told the subconscious mind to be a little bit more patient with the conscious mind, as it's got a lot on at the moment and will get to your requests, but now is not the best time to nag and not care about the dozen other things it has to contend with first.

This is a useful all-purpose technique and it's one that I will ask you to apply frequently in the next two chapters in order to experience for yourself the power of applying some of the approaches that will be covered.

In the next two chapters there will also be much more specific techniques for learning to master your emotional inner self and parts that will allow you to create a healthy whole new relationship with your inner selves.

3 Managing Your Inner Child:
improving your confidence, self-esteem and happiness

'Unless a child has been seen and blessed by another,
it does not exist.'

– Buddhist saying

RMED WITH THE APPROPRIATE ATTITUDES DESCRIBED in the previous chapter, you are now prepared to get down to the actual techniques for managing your subconscious mind.

Managing your self essentially involves working with the three parts of your personality:

- the inner child
- the inner adult
- the inner grandparent

Each one has its own role.

The **inner child** is the client. It is the inner child who has the physical and emotional needs that need to be met. Note that when the inner child is emotionally happy, this spreads to every other aspect of your personality, so that everyone else becomes happy too.

The **inner adult** is responsible for parenting the inner child and making it happy and healthy. It will do this by listening and discerning those needs and then taking appropriate action to meet and balance those needs with others.

The wiser **inner grandparent** is responsible for counselling and advising your inner adult, while at the same time stepping back and allowing the inner adult parent to learn and find their own feet as a parent and manager to self.

Please note that if thinking of yourself as an acting parent to yourself puts you off for any reason, then choose another metaphor you are comfortable with – such as being an executive in charge of a company or a general in charge of an army or whatever works for you.

There are ten important roles and responsibilities the inner adult needs to learn in order to manage the inner child. For ease of reference I will refer to these ten roles collectively as 'self-parenting'. As a consequence of fulfilling these roles, you will see your self-esteem, confidence and well-being soar. The self-parenting roles are:

1. Embrace Your Parenting Role
2. Pay Attention
3. Be a Positive Coach
4. Clarify Needs and Make Good Decisions
5. Validate Your Inner Child
6. Be Responsible For Your Behaviour
7. Be Your Own Inner Advocate
8. Be Your Own Reality Checker
9. Be a Great Problem Solver
10. Discipline With Love

The basic format for self-parenting

I am going to ask you to use the 'meta-mirror-to-self' exercise described at the end of the previous chapter (pages 68–70) as the core system for self-parenting. I will ask you to imagine that you are having a meeting with the three aspects of your personality (inner child, adult and grandparent), each standing at one point of a triangle and then to move your awareness in and out of each one, getting each aspect's take and perspective on things in the process.

With that in place, I am going to ask you to conduct dialogues between them. These dialogues can be conducted silently and mentally in your mind, but I find that it's even more effective and powerful if you state them out loud, because speaking out loud gives weight, recognition and a sense of being witness to your inner thoughts and feelings. In other words, yes, I am asking you to talk to yourself! Have a little fun. If someone walks in, you can tell them that I made you do it and it was not your idea.

You might think at first how weird it feels to be talking to yourself, but we talk, debate and argue with ourselves all the time. Throughout the course of any given day you will variously debate with yourself anything from 'Should I buy this item or not?' or 'What shall I eat tonight?' to any variation of 'Shall I do X or Y?' In the process you will often disagree with yourself and say 'No, I don't want to do that,' or 'I shouldn't have said that/eaten that/done that', etc. All I'm asking you to do is simply make this inner dialogue more formal and explicit so that you become more aware of the communication between your inner selves. It's like asking a person who wants to lose weight to write down what is eaten over the course of a week or month in the form of a food diary. The recorded data often provides a genuine surprise to the client as it reveals what their real relationship with food is, compared to what they think it might be.

In terms of 'how' to actually speak to yourself, it's as simple then as just thinking out loud – just putting into words your actual thoughts and feelings.

To assist you, after explaining each step of the self-parenting process I will be illustrating a mock dialogue between the different parts of your personality, just so you get a sense of the step in action.

Also note that here, at the beginning of this process of self-parenting, I will be asking you to formally step into an aspect of your personality and put into words what you can sense, hear or feel from its perspective. With time and practice, this process becomes speeded up and you will become more intuitive about yourself and your needs. Increasingly you will be able to rely on your intuition more and more and in due course almost be able to jump straight to gut feelings or heartfelt responses and bypass this process altogether. But we have to start with a formal structure until you have practised enough to transcend it.

THE TEN STEPS OF SELF-PARENTING

Step 1: Embrace your parenting role

Bring to mind the meta-mirror-to-self exercise and imagine floating into the inner adult. From its perspective, look at your inner child.

Imagine you can hear the inner grandparent asking you 'And do you [insert your name] undertake to accept this child as your own, as is, warts and all, to look after him or her, to make him or her your priority, to love and cherish your inner child till death do you part?'

As you face the inner child, solemnly vow 'I do'. Then tell the child directly to its face 'And I commit to taking your needs seriously and making you my priority.'

For good measure, the inner grandparent also reminds you that there can never be any refunds or exchanges with your inner child either. This is your inner child assigned to you and no one else.

Undertaking this vow means that you have formally chosen to shift your attention away from fussing over the needs of everyone else's inner children and on to looking after the inner child that you have been entrusted with. It means that you start to take your own needs and your own happiness seriously. That means taking this parenting job seriously because looking after yourself emotionally is what leads to happiness. Your happiness is important and it's up to you to do something about it rather than wait for the day when you've pleased everyone and they give you permission to take the day off and do your own thing. Besides, some people just cannot be pleased and you will never satisfy them no matter how hard you try.

I'd like to congratulate you for taking this healthy step into this new relationship with yourself, but I have to warn you that even if you've taken the right step, don't expect your long-neglected inner child to instantly trust you. Trust has to be earned.

Now float over into the inner-child position and notice

in turn how you feel about your inner adult's vow to you. Your responses may vary from 'Great, let's make up for lost time' to 'Well, this all sounds very nice but don't expect me to forget the neglect of the past three decades, so why should I trust you now? Talk is cheap. Prove it!'

Float back into the inner adult and accept responsibility for the consequences of your past actions. The inner child has the right to feel that way given so many years of being neglected. All you can do to earn that trust is to show that your actions speak louder than words. The remaining nine steps of self-parenting will guide you into just what actions should be. However, it is also up to you to remember that those actions need to be consistent, rather than temporary and cosmetic. It is actions *over time* that are the real proof that you are truly committed to your vow and can in time be trusted.

Step 2: Paying attention

Float into the inner child and consider how you feel about the quality and quantity of attention your inner adult has paid you over the years. To a child, attention means love and care. If you feel that your inner adult has been motivated enough to pay attention to you, you are likely to assume that your inner adult must have done so because he or she cares enough about you to do so. Which implies that if the adult has not been paying enough attention to you, then they must not care about you.

So, for instance, if you feel that your inner adult has seemed mostly distracted and interested in other things, then perhaps you've felt that this must be because you are just too plain dull and uninteresting for even your parent to want to pay attention to you.

Perhaps, deep down, your inner adult does care about you, but has just omitted to give you attention because he or she has been so busy with other things; perhaps it's just because they're a bit clueless about providing attention and didn't know how; perhaps they had the means but just truly did not care enough about you to attend to you. Either way, your self-confidence and self-esteem will have taken a good kicking.

In the real world, lack of good-quality attention from your parent does have reverberations in your later life. Left untreated, as you reach adulthood and desire a partner, you may start assuming that your prospective partner will feel the same way about you that your own parent did (namely that you are not 'good enough' to warrant loving attention). So you become needy, co-dependent and a people pleaser.

Or you may swing the other way and keep ramming evidence of your worth down their throat about what a wacky and interesting person you are, as if you're on a perpetual job interview. Rather perversely, you may end up becoming a bit of a bore about how interesting you are.

Or your confidence may have taken such a knock that you assume no one would be interested in little old you in any case. It's almost as if you are apologetic for the very space you take up on the planet, as if your very existence is selfish and embarrassing because everyone else is more deserving of occupying that space.

In these situations, the lack of loving attention has resulted in either a very shy and reclusive inner child, a rather needy people-pleasing and/or attention-seeking one.

So as the inner chid, what you desire from your inner adult is high-quality attention in a quantity that makes you feel your inner adult must care about you to enough to attend to you so much.

Now float into the inner adult and imagine hearing the grandparent advising you to pay good-quality attention to your inner child, because attention is demonstrating love.

Let's address any ambivalent feelings you may have here. You may think to yourself: 'Okay, I'll look after my inner child since I said I would, but, well, it's just that my inner child seems so shy and dull compared to all the other kids around. I mean look at little Billy or Lucy, who are both so extrovert and outgoing. I wish my one could be more like those kids.' If you feel like this, you are incorrectly assuming that your inner child has no preferences, aptitudes or interests in things in the world and that these other kids do, so your inner child must just be 'boring'. Since he or she is so boring, there's no point engaging with the child or offering it new experiences to try, since boring people aren't interested in those things. You would then find that (rather unsurprisingly), the child doesn't seem to change and continues to be dull. You would then lower your expectations of your child even further and continue to pass him over for further invitations to do new things. All the while you've failed to look at your own parenting role in your child's development. Children start off like clay with huge latent potential to be shaped into any number of wondrous forms. In order to be shaped into something magnificent, they need a lot of parental guidance in the process, just as a beautiful vase doesn't form itself but needs a craftsperson to shape it.

I have met many people who find it easy to show love and care to others but have been unwilling or unable to extend the same level of care to their own inner child. For some it's because they have judged themselves as boring and uninteresting. They fear that if other people got a real glimpse into their true selves, these people would be compelled to run away to prevent them going into some kind of catatonic state. I tell such people that if you want to feel more interesting, then you have to engage your unstimulated emotional self in more interesting things, which means you'll have more interesting things to share with other people.

The inner grandparent advises you to just be a little bit more present, curious and interested in your inner child. The grandparent tells you to observe and notice his or her nature, without any judgement. As you do so, you are likely to start finding out things about him or her that ordinarily you would have overlooked.

For instance, you might say: 'Hmm, I notice that my inner child doodles quite a lot. Maybe he or she's got some artistic merit. Let's investigate that and see what happens.'

So you 'take' him or her to art classes and realise that your child actually quite likes those classes and is even quite good at drawing.

Then you may start to consider: 'Hmm, what else might he or she be interested in? What about books? What kinds of books does he or she like? Well I notice he or she always seems to like reading history and if l look closer I notice he is more focused on the Elizabethan age of England.'

My job as the inner adult is to provide stimulating material for my child's hungry mind, so I buy some more books on this subject area and see what happens. As he or she practically devoured those books, I make a mental note to keep providing books on those subjects as I consider any other things that he or she might also like more of.

What kind of sport might he or she be interested in? Everyone makes a big deal of team sports but I discover that he or she doesn't seem that enthused about them. I've noticed though that he or she has always shown an interest in martial arts films, so I arrange for martial arts classes and see whether that's more in my inner child's interests. Oh look, he or she does shows interest in sports that are more solitary and based on self-development type than team ones, so I make a mental note to pursue more of these kind of sports.

Repeat this process for any area – places to visit, restaurants to go to, people to ask out on a date, etc.

In the process, as the adult, you are learning about your child's preferences, areas of interest that you never noticed before and, if they are healthy preferences, encourage your child to do more of these activities. In fact, simply encouraging healthy activities naturally tends to displace unhealthy ones.

Giving good-quality attention is a bit like providing good-quality listening. Remember the old adage 'You listen but you don't hear?' The ingredients of poor-quality listening apply equally to poor-quality attention. Think of times when you've shown poor-quality listening. What brought on this poor listening? It's the result of your expectations and anticipation about the speaker. In most cases, you would have assumed that the person speaking to you was just not that interesting or had nothing important to say. If this person had nothing of interest to say, it then follows that it would be preferable to focus on your own thoughts and musings and let the other person 'babble away'. You might even make 'polite noises', responding at appropriate moments, but the other person's communication is not really being taken in and processed. It is a form of listening without actually hearing.

On the other hand, when you have listened to somebody that you expected to be interesting, I expect you started off assuming they did have something worthwhile to say, which made you curious about what that might be. You became much more 'present' in the moment and engaged with that person. Even if they haven't said anything 'ground-breaking' in the first ten minutes, you may have maintained an underlying positive assumption – a trust and a faith in that person's potential – to interest you or delight you with their conversation down the line.

What works with others in our relationships works equally well with our inner relationships. Imagine that over a period of weeks you have expressed the same kind of loving attention towards your inner child as you would have to a person you wanted to make friends with. Notice already that you may have softened a bit towards your inner child, perhaps realising that you've been misjudging him or her in the past, but you are delighted and surprised to find those areas of latent potential within him or her that makes him or her more interesting and exciting to be with.

Now float into the inner child across from you and notice what it's like to be on the receiving end of this kind of attention from your adult. What's it like for you when your adult began to let go of their old preconceptions and assumptions about your potential and instead showed more interest and curiosity in things you are interested in? The adult then helped you cultivate those interests and you became more stimulated and excited about having these new activities in your life. You probably feel cared for – which really equates to a feeling of being loved – and is all that you and all children ultimately seek from their parents.

In short, as a result of the process in this step, the inner adult ends up feeling that its emotional inner self is fundamentally interesting and worthy of attention and the inner child starts believing this about themselves too. Confidence and self-esteem begin to rise.

Step 3: Be a positive coach

The best teachers/coaches tend to use praise to encourage their clients; worst ones tend to use criticism. Simply put:

- Descriptive praise **en**-courages (enables courage)
- Unconstructive criticism **dis**-courages (dis-ables courage).

Almost all of my fellow therapists in the UK will tell you that if they were to ask most of their clients to list their faults or things they don't like about themselves on a piece of paper, they would quickly reel off a list of flaws quite easily. When asked instead to do the same for their positive qualities, most seem to struggle and need to be prompted just to write down a few things.

If I were to extrapolate these figures to the general UK population at large, this implies that the country is mostly full of people who are made up of 95 per cent bad qualities and a measly 5 per cent of positive ones. In my experience of living in the UK, the complete opposite has been the case. If you consider the countless thousands of interactions you have had with people in your life, from buying your groceries, tickets, your daily newspaper, waiting in a queue, being at a party, etc., would you say the vast majority of people have acted politely and decently most of the time? They say 'Thank you', 'Sorry' (rather charmingly even if you were to bump into them first); as well as making the ubiquitous comments on the weather and so on. It seems to me most people in the UK are decent and it's only a small minority who seem determined not to be. So what's going on here when all these mostly decent people do not give themselves due credit and praise?

The answer is it's due to negative or critical coaching.

Negative coaching

Negative coaching generally appears in two variations:

DIRECT NEGATIVE COACHING

Imagine floating into the inner-child position and being on the receiving end of the inner adult's coaching style, which seems to have been borrowed from an army drill sergeant – shouting abuse at you, telling you how stupid and what a waste of space you are.

In the army, the sergeant's abusive style is intended to

toughen up recruits for the horror of war. The theory is that recruits need to be exposed to constant stress so that they learn to cope under duress and that if all their flaws are mocked, they will iron them out or risk being shouted at and abused by the sergeant. This strategy may work well for a bunch of steely-eyed men and women who choose arduous training in preparation for fighting for their country, but it's hardly the most constructive approach for coaching your inner child!

This kind of coaching pressure tends to crush the inner child's confidence rather than make them grow strong enough to shrug it off.

INDIRECT ('FRIENDLY') NEGATIVE COACHING

In this case imagine that you, as the inner child, attend a party. You look around at the people present, wondering who you would like to speak to, and then your inner adult takes you aside and says, 'Now, remember, you're not as bright or attractive or as important as everyone else here, so please don't try and talk to them as equals. They are better than you. You will only get disappointed and hurt. Trust me: it's better if you just sat in the corner and tried to not draw attention to yourself.'

Friendly negative coaching is like a nasty little Trojan horse virus that is couched in a blanket of caring. The care wrapped around the message deceives our normal defence radar that would otherwise operate when people are being mean to us and sneaks the Trojan horse right through. We're more likely to take things to heart when someone kindly and helpfully takes us aside to offer us some friendly advice, as our guard is down and we are more vulnerable to the subsequent 'helpful' character assassination.

Why negative coaching does not work

I've yet to come across a patient of mine who has responded with the criticism they faced from their parents by punching the air and saying 'Thank you so much, Mum and Dad, for your endless criticism of my shortcomings. You have made me the incredibly secure and confident person I am today.'

It sounds ludicrous, doesn't it, and yet why are otherwise intelligent people still 'helping' their children to become more confident using harsh criticism?

All too often the way children tend to actually react to relentless criticism can be summed up in the words of one of my patients: 'I'd flinch whenever Mother called my name because of her constant criticism. Nothing I did was ever right. Whenever she talked to me it was to tell me I'd done something wrong.' The anxiety my patient felt ended up interfering and distracting him from learning other things.

In my own life I had a similar experience with my first maths teacher. As a result, other than basic arithmetic, I have a real block when it comes to maths. Note that in school I was in the highest percentile for every subject *except* maths, so it couldn't be excused away on the basis that I was thick. There was something very specific about maths. When I was first learning maths, at a formative, impressionable age, my maths teacher would go about explaining some new mathematical problem and, if I or another student did not immediately understand this information or answer his questions correctly, my maths teacher would get very cross and pinch or cuff us and we got very scared. It was hard enough trying getting to grips with English as my second language, let alone the peculiar language of maths. From my maths teacher's point of view, I expect he was thinking, 'If other kids can get this straight off, then everyone should, so if he is not answering the questions correctly, then he *must* be just lazy.' In which case it would have made sense to him to 'punish' students.

Of course it is very hard to solve a problem one is already struggling with when you are also fearing the equivalent of an electric shock when you are trying to think. When the 'helpful' advice: 'You'll always be bad at maths', was added to the mix by my maths teacher, I took it as a statement of fact from a figure in authority and so a belief that I was bad at maths was soon created which stayed even after I left my first school.

So the bottom-line result was that critical coaching merely served to undermine any developing confidence I had in the subject and discouraged me from seeking to get better at it and the effects were long-lasting and detrimental. Great job of getting people proficient in maths, Mr Maths Teacher!

So if there is any part of you that still thinks that criticising yourself or others in order to help and motivate them by fear, shame, embarrassment and threats works, then please, please start being irreverent to these notions. While there might be some short-term gains from using shame and fear, in my experience the long-term effect is always undermining. It causes neuroses (a neurotic desire to people-please and make amends), perfectionism (which can lead to depression) or rebellious behaviour (leading to self-sabotage and missed potential).

In contrast, let's look to examples of where coaching has been effective and produced results. The most obvious area is with babies and infants. Babies and infants are the best learners on the planet because, in a very short space of time, they are learning a language at the same time as learning to walk, jump and imitate dozens of other gestures and what helps them achieve this is the style of positive coaching that they receive. For instance, every time our daughter Lara did something or imitated something, regardless of how imperfectly reproduced, my wife and I would be having kittens, calling the other one over, smiling back at Lara, cuddling, kissing and generally gushing over the achievement. If you think about it from my daughter's point of view, she is on the receiving end of this wonderful attention and praise. So she is very highly motivated to repeat the cute phrase she just said or to take another little jump or skip and receive yet more positive reinforcement.

In many, many families, it seems that this effective method of positive reinforcement for encouraging a child to try new things simply stops one day. In its place, parents begin to take the child's achievements as a given. Their feedback towards their child becomes confined to only pointing out only the child's shortcomings and failings. I have personally heard several patients tell me that they got between 97 to 98 per cent on a maths exam and their parent only responded by saying: 'What about the other 2 per cent you got wrong?'

Granted that from the parent's point of view, as the child gets older, it is expected that it should become competent in many things and as such not deserving of any special praise, in the same that I don't praise my four-year-old daughter for walking or running any more. I just expect her to do so. However, I do continue to praise her for new things she is learning. In other cases I have seen, some parents take it to another level by only 'helpfully' pointing out (criticising) the areas where the child is still imperfect. Perfection becomes the new minimum standard of achievement.

Switching from positive coaching to critical coaching aiming at perfectionism must appear very confusing to the child as it is a complete role-reversal to what he or she has been used to experiencing before. At one point, the child had a motivation system of learning, whereby it could do no wrong whenever it tried. Then suddenly it changed to a system whereby no matter how hard that child tries to learn a new skill, unless it is quickly perfected, the child comes in for a barrage of criticism.

Moreover, since parents act as role models for children, as kids we tend to 'internalise' their comments, just as if we were to record their remarks on a little CD player in our head that then plays those comments on a continuous background loop. So we end up becoming our own negative coaches even when our parents are not around or long gone.

Positive coaching

The simple antidote to critical coaching is positive coaching – the same kind of coaching that we started off applying to babies and infants. After all, in many ways teenagers and adults continue to be simply 'big children'. We adults are also trying to operate in a world, albeit a more complex one, which we do not fully understand or comprehend. Pretty much all that has changed is that we have grown bigger physically and our problems are more complex, but the principles still remain the same as they did when we were babies. There is no age or height restriction to the benefits of praise, understanding, tolerance and compassion.

There are three important elements to positive coaching:

1. A focus on 'process', not 'outcome'

When you see children drawing something like a house with Mummy and Daddy, they don't stop and say to themselves, 'Look at my drawing, those stick figures look nothing like Mum and Dad. I'm rubbish at drawing and should quit now to avoid embarrassment.' Children don't fret that they can't read their whole bedtime book yet or that they can't remember all the moves of a school dance. It doesn't put them off drawing or reading or dancing. They don't beat themselves up and think of themselves as failures.

Why is this? Well, at some level children realise that they've embarked on a learning *process*. There's no actual defined end point to judge oneself against as good or bad. The process never ends. As soon as you master one book, you start reading one with slightly harder words. Young children will internalise this useful 'process-orientated' approach until we adults helpfully talk them out of it and teach them an outcome-orientated approach.

In contrast adults are very outcome-orientated, which means that when adults do not reach their desired outcome (usually an unrealistic or overly ambitious goal), they immediately think in terms of success or failure, even if what they achieved was still impressive in its own right. Rather ironically, children are demonstrating a more mature enjoyment of the spirit of the exercise rather than a fixation on one transient point on that process. Children display a playful, experimental, fun and curious approach, and that is exactly the kind of environment where learning and creativity flower most, not just for children, but also for most adults.

Here's a famous example: following his outstanding contribution to the development of the atom bomb in the Second World War, 27-year-old Richard Feynman became Professor of Theoretical Physics at Cornell University. Feynman was given a huge salary and expected to follow in the great footsteps of other contemporary physicists such as Einstein. The interesting thing is that this brilliant young man suffered a complete 'writer's block' whenever he faced the daunting challenge of delivering an outcome worthy of his position. He considered the reasons for his creative block and realised it was because physics had stopped being fun and had become a chore. It had been fun when he was curious about things and when physics was seen as a learning process about the world around him. So he decided to follow his curiosity and make it fun again. A few days later he was in the canteen and saw some students fooling around and throwing a spinning plate in the air. Feynman observed the plate wobble and spin and he started scribbling down equations concerning the relation between wobble and spin. When he mentioned his findings to another colleague, his colleague chided him for wasting his time on such trivial matters when he should be focusing on achieving great things instead. Feynman wasn't discouraged and afterwards said it was like 'uncorking a bottle' where everything flowed out effortlessly. Incidentally, his diagrams about wobbling plates led to him winning the Nobel Prize for Physics.

So as the inner adult observes the developmental path of your inner child, remember that your inner child is on a learning curve, rather than on a fixed outcome. Some things they will learn relatively quickly, other things relatively slowly. It's not meant to be a race. It takes what it takes for the child to learn something and the best thing you can do is be patient and supportive so that what needs to be learnt will be learnt as speedily as possible without unhelpful distractions and negative speculation about their 'true' potential.

2. Proactive encouragement

The inner adult doesn't have to wait for something to go wrong before offering support and sympathy. They can take a proactive approach and encourage children about experiences before they experiment with them. Most children are naturally cautious and conservative about new experiences because they don't have any historical precedents to gauge whether they would enjoy the experience or not. They need someone to say, 'Go on, I think you'll be really good at this.' Adults need to be leaders because children take their cue from their parents' leads.

Sometimes the inner child just needs a little pep talk. Nerves and anticipatory anxiety may get the better of a child occasionally. Even seasoned athletes and performers experience moments of panic and doubt before a performance. If even experienced grown men and women are allowed to have crisis of confidence attacks, then one should be even more understanding and sympathetic to a child who is younger, less experienced and less confident. What is not very helpful is the inner adult reacting to these moments of crises with, 'Oh God, here we go again. Why can't you be like everyone else'.

SELF-PEP TALK

1. Get in the constructive frame of mind.
2. When a crisis of confidence occurs, immediately imagine the inner grandparent advising you to keep calm and accept that your inner child is having a crisis and needs you to offer him or her a pep talk. Put your metaphorical 'encouraging hat' on.
3. Calm yourself down first so you can then help your inner child.
4. Take a few deep breaths and imagine the stress being earthed and discharged through the soles of your feet. When we are calm we operate more from the pre-frontal cortex thinking brain rather than the more panicky, reactive emotional limbic brain.
5. Offer the inner child a pep talk.
6. 'Hey it's normal to feel scared or doubtful; even seasoned pros feel scared before such events. You're just feeling a little spooked right now, that's all, but remember that the other person or team is also feeling the same way about competing with you. All you need to focus on is just making the best attempts you can today and that's all one can ask. Have a little fun and forget about everything else in the process.'

3. Post-experience descriptive praise

It's important to 'debrief' the inner child immediately after it's had an experience, especially a new one, because the child may create a strong belief about that experience, which could be positive or negative. You have a short window of opportunity to fill the vacuum of information about the experience to create a positive 'template', such as 'You show real promise in skiing.'

Descriptive praise offers the child *evidence* of its capability, promise and potential. Non-descriptive praise (e.g. 'Well, I think you're amazing at football') can sound hollow, ill-defined and insincere. The child is likely to think 'Of course you would say that, you're my parent, but is it true?' Descriptive praise instead actually describes the reasons meriting praise, so that the child realises there is a rationale behind being praised, so it readily accepts the praise offered.

In order to offer descriptive praise, stand back and consider the whole process of the experience your inner child went through and remember to treat it as a learning curve (rather than a definitive outcome of your child's abilities). Then review the areas that are worth singling out for praise where the child showed potential and describe them to him or her. This is not just for sporting events but anything they managed well e.g. 'I'm very proud of you for keeping your cool even when the other person was deliberately provoking you.'

If after the experience, constructive criticism is called for, then it's possible to express both descriptive praise and constructive criticism using a format called the feedback sandwich.

The Feedback Sandwich

It is known as a sandwich because, just as a sandwich has a slice of bread, then the filling and then bread again, the feedback sandwich starts with a layer of descriptive praise, has a middle layer of constructive feedback and finishes with another layer of praise.

An example might go: 'Jane, I'm really proud of what a great job you did with this dinner party, making so many tasty dishes, especially the fish, which was completely new to you. What could make it even better next time is to reduce the salt and add more lemon to the salad, as it took away a little bit from the soup, but all in all it was a raging success and all the guests had a great time.'

The feedback sandwich also allows a fairer picture by balancing out the 'negatives' with the positives also present.

Positive coaching with mirror for self

Float into the inner adult and imagine practising positive coaching, descriptive praise or the feedback sandwich. Notice that as you do so, you feel more like a mentor than a critic. You are more focused on your protégé's learning curve rather than getting fixated on specific outcomes. That allows you to relax and engage in the experience itself more.

Then float into the inner child and imagine that for several weeks your adult has been praising you for things you are learning to do. What does it feel like to be encouraged and motivated in this way? Even when some criticism is called for, it's done in a way that inspires you to try things again.

On the whole you find that you become more motivated to pursue the activities your adult is encouraging you to do. Consequently, your faith and confidence in your abilities, and yourself in general, grows more and more. The more confident you feel, the more belief you have in yourself. The more belief you have in yourself, the more motivated you are to try things and the better results you will get. The better results you get, the more your confidence grows and the more you believe in yourself and the more successful you will become in your life in general. Much success in life (job interviews, dating, networking, asking for a promotion, offering a service or a product) comes from an intangible aspect like confidence. Being a positive coach to yourself is one of the most powerful ways for you to internalise deep-rooted self-confidence and self-belief.

Step 4: Clarify needs and make good decisions

Why should you want to become better at making decisions for yourself?

Well, put it this way: where you are in your life generally – your health, your wealth, your relationships – and your overall success, depends upon the sum total of all the decisions you have made (or not made) for yourself. The more decisions you make, the more experiences you will pack into your life and the richer your life will be and the more you will feel you 'lived' life.

The more indecisive you are, the fewer decisions you will make, the fewer experiences you will have, the more impoverished your life will feel. You might end up feeling as if you are 'existing' rather than really living. Decision-making is like a muscle. The more you train it, the better you will get at taking decisions.

In theory, decision-making and exercising this muscle should be simple.

For the sake of argument, let's start with talking about simple everyday decisions one might need to make. Suppose you are presented with a choice of very different foods or different clothes or you need to choose from different birthday cards or whatever. How do you choose between them?

The choice you will make must depend upon you satisfying some sort of personal criteria or checklist for those things – i.e. your *values* around those items. What you 'value' in things could be anything from buying products based purely on pragmatic grounds to buying completely impractical things, purely on aesthetic grounds. The point is, when you know what your values about something are, it's easy to make decisions in your selections because you just need to bring up your values checklist, compare them to the items available and then the product with the most ticks for your selection criteria wins.

By the same token, if you are unclear about your values around about a selection of things you need to choose from, then how will you know which items to pick? You won't know when you are satisfying your criteria or not. Consequently, you might end up dithering and avoiding making any kind of decision, which can make you feel that you are indecisive. However, just because you've ended up sitting on the fence on making decisions in these areas, doesn't actually mean you are indecisive per se. I expect if I won the lottery and offered you ten thousand pounds to sing 'Happy Birthday' to me on the spot, you wouldn't be racked with indecision and need to debate within yourself about whether you should sing or go shopping instead. You'd sing like a little canary with a big fat smile on your face. Making a quick decision and taking appropriate action here would be incredibly easy because you are clear about your input and your desired outcome.

The trick to becoming more decisive therefore is to *clarify* your values in the choices you are faced with.

Some decisions can be made purely on pragmatic terms through some kind of logical process of elimination e.g. if you are choosing a computer you'd think about which computer offers you the best relative price or RAM capacity or will fit on your desk. Choices based on pragmatic values tend to be made by the conscious mind, since logic is the realm of the left brain and conscious mind. But what about choices where pragmatism isn't a consideration and instead it's more just a question of preference, e.g. choosing between one coloured wallpaper and another of the same price? Decisions made here will depend on your feelings and emotions, i.e. your *emotional values* around those things. Your emotional values are contained in your emotional self, which is the inner child part of your personality. Again, your inner child will have preferences for choices for many things when questioned. It's just that it's not often asked what its preferences are and then that can come across as if it doesn't have any preferences in the first place. As mentioned earlier, this is misleading; preferences may well exist but are just not being accessed and elicited.

Eliciting emotional values

Let's start with using a simple example of eliciting your inner preferences about things, such as feeling hunger and deciding what food you are going to eat.

INNER CHILD: Hunger, hunger!
INNER ADULT: What kind of hunger is that? A hunger for what kind of food?

Notice we've done away with the old 'just eat this and do what you're told, I haven't got time for you' approach. Now we are using an open-ended question to elicit more feedback to make the most appropriate decision.

INNER CHILD: Gee I've no idea. It's been so long since I was actually asked that I've completely fallen out of the habit of knowing what I want.
INNER ADULT: Okay, well let me help you. Of your favourite foods that I can provide for you – Italian, French, Spanish, Chinese, Thai – which do you lean towards most?

The adult now tunes in and listens to the *feedback* from the subconscious mind. 'Feedback' is essentially listening to *information.* 'Information' in turn is just fundamentally *news of difference.* News of difference is essentially *discerning even a slight preference for one thing* more than another.

So the inner adult is looking to detect even just that smallest preference for one food option over another.

INNER ADULT: Well, I've noticed that you're pausing longer over the Italian food option, as if hoping that someone will pick it for you, so I'll pick it for you and let's start with that.

An aside

Have you ever had the experience of being in a situation where somebody says to you 'Do you prefer option A or B?' and you say, 'I don't mind, whichever', but inside you think *'But I hope it's option A?'* Why don't we simply just say we would prefer option A? Why even entertain that 50:50 chance when we could guarantee the outcome with a simple few words? It's the job of the conscious mind, in its active executive role, to get the best option to match the preferences of its 'client'. It needs to respond more proactively to such situations by saying, 'I'd prefer option A please, Bob.'

Now that the inner adult has selected the option of 'Italian food' on behalf of the inner child, the process doesn't end there until there is a specific, concrete end point. So the inner adult continues to repeat this cycle of trying to discern what the inner child wants.

> INNER ADULT: And of the Italian options available on this menu – pizza or pasta – do you prefer more pizza or more pasta? Again, the conscious mind listens to the feedback from that, looking for that slight preference for one option more than another.
>
> INNER CHILD: Hmm, I like both pizza and pasta.
>
> INNER ADULT: Sure you do. Can we have both? Hmm, no, there's no combo plate, so which one do you have the slightest preference for right now? You can always have the other one next time.
>
> INNER CHILD: Hmm, I guess the pizza.
>
> INNER ADULT: Okay, let's go with that.

We still don't know what kind of pizza is preferred, so the process continues:

> INNER ADULT: And of pizza, do you prefer more meat or more vegetable pizza?
>
> INNER CHILD: I guess ones with vegetables for a change.
>
> INNER ADULT: Okay, the options are ones with cheese, mushrooms, artichokes or courgettes. Which one do you prefer most?
>
> INNER CHILD: Hmm, maybe the one with artichokes.
>
> INNER ADULT: Okay, that's a *quattro stagione*, so I'll get us that.

You started off with something vague like 'hunger' and ended with something specific such as 'pizza *quattro stagione*'.

It's not something you could jump straight to. You had to go through a inner process of:

- listening to your inner feelings and needs
- being responsible for meeting those needs
- then presenting options that could meet those needs
- then selecting one of those options and then continuing to subdivide those sub-options until there were no further options and a natural end point in the decision-making process was reached.

Using hunger as an example may sound simple compared to more complex emotional needs, but the same process still works even for more complex needs. For example:

INNER CHILD: Stress, stress!

INNER ADULT: What kind of stress is that?

INNER CHILD: Gee, I don't know...

INNER ADULT: [comparing and contrasting] Well is it too little of something (e.g. sleep, play) or too much of something (e.g. work)?

INNER CHILD: Hmm, I feel it's a 'less of something'.

INNER ADULT: What kind of less? Regarding what?

INNER CHILD: I guess I just feel fed up.

INNER ADULT: Okay you feel fed up, what kind of fed up is that fed up, just so I know?

INNER ADULT: I guess I'm bored.

INNER ADULT: Okay, so it's a bored fed-upness. Sounds like 'un-stimulated'?

INNER CHILD: Yeah, I feel really un-stimulated.

INNER ADULT: [identified unmet need, can now switch to

solution mode] So if you had something stimulating to do, would that clear up the problem for you?

INNER CHILD: Yeah I think so.

INNER ADULT: [now knows the goal] Okay, so of the options for stimulation I can provide sporting, musical, internet, books, talking to a friend, video game – which do you prefer most right now?

The inner adult again tunes in to listen, subdividing the options based on feedback until there is a specific end point, e.g.:

INNER CHILD: A book.

INNER ADULT: Okay a book. Which genre?

INNER CHILD: Escapism and adventure.

INNER ADULT: Okay, fiction, non-fiction, historical fiction, crime, sci-fi?

INNER CHILD: Hmm, sci-fi!

INNER ADULT: Okay, let's look at the selection of books on the sci-fi shelf.

End point reached.

This same process can be substituted for the subjects of career or romantic partner or anything else.

Using the mirror to self-format again, float into the inner child and consider how it feels to be consulted in this way. If you feel your needs are being taken more seriously, you begin to take them more seriously too, rather than feeling other people's preferences are more important than yours. Over time you begin to have more trust and faith in your adult to listen, understand and meet your physical and emotional needs, which also makes you feel more 'secure' in general. Since your needs are being met, that means you are becoming less 'needy'. With your needs being looked after in safe hands, you can relax more, enjoy life and engage in other more pleasurable pursuits.

Wider self-management implications

The inner adult has to discern and clarify other emotional needs in addition to those mentioned. These can be thought of as part of the inner adult's general management responsibilities. So what are these other needs that the inner adult has to be aware of?

Psychologist Joe Griffin and Ivan Tyrell[5] propose that our basic emotional needs are as follows:

- **Security** — safe territory and an environment which allows us to develop fully
- **Attention** (to give and receive it)
- **Sense of autonomy and control** – having volition to make responsible choices
- Being **emotionally connected** to others
- **Feeling part of a wider community**
- **Friendship, intimacy** – to know that at least one other person accepts us totally for who we are, 'warts 'n' all'
- **Privacy** – opportunity to reflect and consolidate experience

---

5 Joe Griffin & Ivan Tyrell (2003): *Human Givens: A New Approach to Emotional Health & Clear Thinking*

- **Sense of status** within social groupings
- **Sense of competence and achievement**
- **Meaning and purpose** – which come from being stretched in what we do and think.

Griffin and Tyrell suggest that good health in any living organism is essentially the result of all its physical and emotional needs being met in balance. When all the organisms' needs are in balance, then the organism thrives. When the needs are not balanced, the organism suffers.

In self-parenting terms we can simplify this to mean that the inner child has all these aforementioned emotional needs which need to be balanced and the inner adult is in charge of discerning these needs and meeting them in the appropriate balance. What prevents these needs not being met is mostly the quality of the relationship between the inner adult and the inner child as discussed (judgements, lack of empathy, misunderstanding and miscommunication). As you improve the quality of the relationship between these two aspects of yourself, then it clears the road for your inner adult to pursue these needs in a healthy way without obstructions or distractions.

In addition, with the list of the above emotional needs, your inner adult has a ready checklist of emotional needs in place that it needs to fulfil. Your inner adult can now go through the list, comparing and contrasting and ask:

INNER ADULT: [to inner child] Do you feel your friendship needs are being met in balance or do you want me to make more friends for you? Do you feel sufficiently stretched and challenged at work or do you want me to explore new options for you?

Such a road map of needs allows your inner adult to become more preventative and proactive in pursing your emotional needs, not just reacting to discontent after the impact of the need not being met in the first place.

Step 5: Validate your inner child

I already spoke about *what* validation is in Chapter 2 and how our subconscious mind needs to feel validated in order for it to process feelings and emotions. This step here will cover *how* to validate your inner child in more detail.

Validating your inner child entails a similar process to the clarifying preferences for decision-making shown in the previous step, except with much more of a focus on validation of important underlying feelings rather than the preferences themselves. The formula for successful validation is:

Validate–validate–validate–lead (to a solution).

Note that sometimes it's not always necessary to have to lead to a solution. More often than not, simply validating what your inner child feels is itself the solution. I suspect that many times you've gone to your partner or family upset about an event and your nearest and dearest have jumped to telling you solutions when you are very well aware of them, but that's not what you want from your family. You want them to listen so that you can take stock of what's bothering you and that itself is the process that processes your unresolved emotions. That itself is the solution.

Note also that ALL feelings should be validated, regardless of their magnitude and importance. Remember the motto of the subconscious mind is 'you can only feel what you feel'.

Here is an illustration of validation and leading to a solution-in-action:

INNER ADULT: [noticing a distressed look on the inner child's face] Hey, what's up?

INNER CHILD: I think I'm sad, but I shouldn't feel sad, I mean it's a nice day and I've got a good life and there are so many unfortunate people in the world who are experiencing real hardship...

INNER ADULT: [ignoring any mention of the right or wrongs of being sad and just focusing on what is] Okay, you feel sad. Just allow yourself to feel this feeling without judgement. And, just so I know, what's the specific aspect you are sad about?

INNER CHILD: [tunes into the emotion more] I guess I'm lonely.

INNER ADULT: Okay, you're feeling sad because you're lonely? And what's the specific sadness with being lonely for you, just so I'm clear?

INNER CHILD: I've got no one to talk to.

INNER ADULT: Okay, I'm getting it, so the specific aspect you feel sad about is having no one to talk to, is that right?

INNER CHILD: [thinking about it] Yes.

INNER ADULT: [switching to solution mode] So if you had

someone to talk to, that you would like to talk to, would you still be sad?

INNER CHILD: [thinks about it] I guess not.

INNER ADULT: [seeking more specificity by comparing and contrasting] So are you looking for something romantic or platonic?

INNER CHILD: [thinks about it] I guess I just need a friend.

INNER ADULT: Okay, one friend or many?

INNER CHILD: Just one will do.

INNER ADULT: Male of female?

INNER CHILD: Female.

INNER ADULT: How old?

INNER CHILD: Ideally my age, give or take a few years.

INNER ADULT: Okay, for what purpose do you really want a female friend of your age?

INNER CHILD: I really want someone to share going to the theatre with and other local events.

Once the real unmet emotional need had been found, the inner adult can put on their brainstorming hat and do a Google search for opera appreciation societies, finding one, posting on its noticeboard (such as 'looking for fellow theatre lover') and looking for people who are in the same boat.

At the start of this conversation, it was not at all obvious that the real underlying reason for the inner child's sadness was that she missed going to the opera, in the same way that it was not obvious that a signal for hunger ends up leading to choosing a pizza *quattro stagione*, in the decision-making step mentioned earlier. It wasn't even obvious to the inner child herself until she engaged in some kind of validation and clarification process led by the inner adult.

If instead of using the validation–validation–validation–lead, the inner adult had used the all too common 'no-validation-jump-to-lead' then the process might have taken a very different direction and gone something like this:

> INNER ADULT: [noticing a distressed look on the inner child's face] Hey, what's up?
>
> INNER CHILD: I think I'm sad, but I shouldn't feel sad, I mean it's a nice day and I've got a good life and there are so many unfortunate people in the world who are experiencing real hardship…
>
> INNER ADULT: [wanting to ignoring any undesired 'negativity' and wanting to force premature positivity] Don't feel sad; it's a beautiful day, you're only 30, why don't you go shopping? That will make you feel better.

That sounds like a useful approach on the face of it but it would keep missing the underlying unmet need. If my grandmother complained of not feeling well when the real unmet need is that she wanted attention (but does not know how to ask for it), then rushing in to give her medicine is not what is actually needed and might makes things worse. And at the same time the real need remains unresolved and continues to 'act out'.

Many therapies and self-help books out there are teaching people to dismiss negativity and jump to the 'positive' solution. These approaches are overly upbeat and invalidating because responding to someone's distress by jumping to 'solutions' is a form of denying those feelings and jams their very processing. So if you have been exposed to such approaches, remember to add the crucial steps of validation first. You will reach your desired outcome, but just honour each stage of the process on the way.

So I'm hoping that you're beginning to see that all the steps so far interweave and build on each other. Clarification and validation go hand in hand, as do coaching and decision-making. The main element I'd like to emphasise in this self-parenting step is the attitude of listening *without judgement or criticism*. Your focus of attention at this point should be on the inner child's experience, rather than the rights or wrongs of the details of that experience. In the recent example the inner child was unable to validate herself because she had problems accepting her feelings in the first place. She felt she had no right to complain or feel bad about anything when most people in the world are facing harder problems. Not accepting her feelings blocked her from pursuing those sad feelings to find the real underlying unmet need.

As the inner adult you could have also clarified and validated her feelings further at this point by adding: 'I know you feel guilty because you feel sad over something that in *absolute* terms is not a minor problem, but in *relative* terms, missing the opera was a big deal for you and we live in a relative world and that's just how it is. Insisting on being sad and foregoing your own emotional needs doesn't make the poor of the world any happier.'

In fact, rather perversely, the inner child may feel forced to raise the stakes in order to be acknowledged. For instance, if the inner child feels it doesn't have the right to a feeling, it can respond with: 'Well, if no one it taking my sadness seriously, then maybe if I had a "proper depression", that would prove that this is not a silly problem, but a real issue for me.' As such, some people unwittingly create a depressive mindset for themselves just by expecting that their feelings will be belittled or dismissed (i.e. not accepted) by others.

Now using the meta-mirror for self, switch into the inner child's perspective and imagine starting off experiencing some form of distress and having your inner adult respond to you in this validating approach instead. How might that feel to have your feelings honoured, respected and taken seriously? There would be no more need to fight, defend or justify your right to feel what you feel.

Another added benefit of this process is that it would teach you to be more accountable, in touch and responsible for your feelings, so you 'own' them, to use a term from psychotherapy.

Step 6: Be responsible for your behaviour

One of the tasks a parent has to teach their child is to develop a sense of personal responsibility, to consider and accept the consequences of their actions. As children we start off with the experience that our needs are someone else's problem. As we grow older, we become more responsible for considering what we want and then doing something about it, rather than continuing to expect others to do this for us.

All too often, the inner child in us continues to want something without considering the larger consequences.

Since the inner adult is the one who is aware of such consequences – whether it's health and safety or the need for
prudent budgeting for non-emergency items – the inner
adult has a reflexive tendency to say 'no' first, to create
space to deliberate the pros and cons of its decision. In other
words, it's demonstrating to the inner child that 'no means
maybe' or 'don't take no for an answer'.

So the inner child thinks this is a game – an adversarial
game involving persisting until someone blinks first and
caves in. And so the conscious and subconscious minds
unwittingly fall into a general adversarial relationship, rather
like the relationship between Britain's two main political
parties. Often, whenever one party proposes a policy, the
other party resists or criticises it on principle, rather than
admit any merit in the other's point. The inner child sees its
role as that of lobbying for a desired item, then expecting the
inner adult to adopt the polar opposite position (to resist
buying that item), which means the inner child prepares to
stick to its guns with persistent, intense nagging. Consequently,
the clarity between 'needing' something and 'wanting' it
becomes the first casualty of this war. The inner child
becomes focused on *wanting* something rather than whether
it *needs* that thing or not. This is why we are often exasperated with ourselves for buying stuff we simply do not need or
barely use.

There's another important reason why your inner child
can seem so unfeasibly stubborn and defiant to your wishes
and it's due to what's called the oppositional reflex.
Knowing how the oppositional reflex and the adversarial
game works will help us play these games better and lead
ourselves towards a healthy win–win outcome.

The oppositional reflex

The oppositional reflex works like this: children have a strong innate need for autonomy – for increasingly more say and input in their lives. For instance, I used to watch my young son Jamie trying to feed himself and noticed that half the food would find its way to his mouth and the rest would fall on his lap, whereby he would then try and pick it up, thus doubling his workload. My watching inner adult would want to improve Jamie's intake by taking the spoon and feeding him in mouthfuls so all the food went neatly into his mouth. Was he grateful to me for at a stroke doubling his efficiency? No, he started yelling at me because he wanted the spoon back so he could continue to feed himself.

Normally children will instinctively fight any perceived attempts to control their natural healthy expression of independence because children want to learn to do things for themselves. This is a good thing as it makes them strive for independence and move away from being overly dependant on others. However, we parents often don't have the time nor the inclination to sit patiently, while feeding time takes twice as long with ten times the mess, so we may start to control matters and insist on feeding our child. If we succumb to our quest for efficiency, the child starts to believe that it will always need to fight others for its right to independence. Years later as an adult, an individual may still instinctively resist anyone trying to tell it what to do, even if that advice is really helpful and profitable. Such a person is more interested in making sure he or she is preserving their independence than in making life smoother, more efficient, healthier or richer.

Our inner child behaves exactly in this same way with its inner parent. If the inner child has developed a strong oppositional reflex, then any attempts to force it to change will be doomed. Fighting it head-on would never work. Another tactic would be needed to get it to let go of its unhelpful behaviour and choose something better in its place. That tactic requires stepping out of the old tyrant-boss role of 'do what I say because I'm the boss' and back to the coach-facilitator role.

Here's a typical scenario from my life to illustrate the before-and-after approach:

WHAT NOT TO DO

INNER CHILD: Ooh, look at that new gadget, want it, want it...

INNER ADULT: Well you can't have it. You don't need it.

INNER CHILD: [seeing this as a contest of wills, gets into lobbying-for-gadgets mode] Want it... want it... want it...want it...

INNER ADULT: [eventually becomes so worn down or fed up] Okay, have your damn gadget. You're driving me crazy.

INNER CHILD: Memo to self: remember to treat this as an endurance test and if I pester him long enough, he'll change his mind, so don't listen when he says 'no'.

WHAT TO DO INSTEAD

Instead of falling into the old contest-of-wills game, the inner adult sidesteps this old pattern and understands that its job is to lead the inner child to becoming more *accountable* for what it actually wants. A new encounter might now proceed as follows instead:

INNER CHILD: Ooh, new computer, want it, want it.

INNER ADULT: Okay, well if you need it, I will get it for you. [It's very hard to resist someone who agrees with you.] But before I do that, I just want to clarify a couple of things. How much is this new computer?

INNER CHILD: Two thousand pounds.

INNER ADULT: Okay and do we have two thousand pounds?

INNER CHILD: Yes, want it, want it.

INNER ADULT: Okay, before we spend it, is there anything else we want to buy that's really expensive?

INNER CHILD: Yes, a holiday.

INNER ADULT: Okay and how much is the holiday?

INNER CHILD: Um, also two thousand pounds.

INNER ADULT: Fine, so do we have four thousand pounds to spend on both?

INNER CHILD: Uh, no.

INNER ADULT: How much do we have?

INNER CHILD: Just two thousand pounds.

INNER ADULT: Okay, so we can only get just one of those choices. Which one is more important to you: a new computer or that holiday?

INNER CHILD: Well, I was looking forward to the holiday and I already have a computer, so I guess the holiday more.

INNER ADULT: You sure?

INNER CHILD: Yeah, the holiday.

INNER ADULT: Okay, but only if you really want it.'

It is possible to end up with the inner child itself insisting it wants to save money or pursue some other more sensible option, rather than having to always fight tooth and nail for every inch of progress as with the old system. The key is to draw the inner child's attention back to its wider values, while keeping a cool head, regardless of background stress and not reacting emotionally to the apparent selfishness of the inner child (children are by nature 'self-centred' anyway). Keeping calm allows you to 'work the system' rather than reacting or getting drawn back into the old adversarial conflict of 'want vs don't want'.

Meta-mirror for self

Float back into the inner child and get a sense of what it feels like now when you know your feelings and desires are taken seriously rather than being instantly vetoed and told no out of hand.

The fact that you do not always get your initial 'want' is not actually what is important to you. It's that you feel respected and are shown, without any pressure, an alternative path where your needs are considered and explored and your ultimate decision also respected. The respect shown throughout this approach means that you will be more inclined to reciprocate and cooperate and meet the inner adult halfway. You've now entered into a more mature relationship based more on negotiation among equals rather than demanding and throwing one's weight about. Another happy by-product is that you will be spending your money more wisely on what is needed rather than just wanted.

Step 7: Be your own inner advocate

This is a natural aspect of the inner adult that can be accessed when called for. Think of a dedicated and fearless lawyer who is prepared to do anything to support or defend his or her client, no matter how daunting and powerful the people he or she is up against – that's the kind of advocate role I'm talking about. This kind of advocate never sells out his client but stands loyally and steadfastly with them.

In the previous step I talked about the oppositional reflex – an instinctive behaviour designed to protect our autonomy, free will and choice. The part of us that opposes any perceived attempt to control us or have our choices curtailed is our own natural inner advocate. However, the kind of inner advocate involved in this oppositional reflex is usually young and immature and so overzealous and militant in the pursuit of the principles of ensuring free will that he often ends up opposing options that would benefit his client. The more mature and sophisticated inner advocate wisely knows that long-term success requires building bridges and coalitions. He does not blindly fight and antagonise everyone around him just on the assumption that everyone else is out to take away his client's freedom of choice. The mature advocate has his sights on the bigger win–win situation that honours everyone where possible. Needless to say, if push were to come to shove and only a win–lose outcome were on the table, the mature inner advocate has no qualms about winning the case for his client, even if others must lose and suffer. Rather them than his client.

Let's say my parents have their heart set on me training to be a solicitor, whereas I want to train as a psychologist. It seems inevitable that someone is going to be disappointed and it's the job of my inner advocate to make sure that it is not his/her client that is the one disappointed. It's not easy going against one's parents as they often know which heartstrings to pull, but what helps our inner advocate to do so is by remaining focused on the bottom-line, defending his client's 'brief' (of wanting to train in psychology). If he failed to do this and caved in or 'bought into' any of the tactics used by my parents, then to all intents and purposes he would have 'sold out' to another client and that's dereliction of duty.

Case study: Sara's inner advocate

Sara is an attractive West Indian lady in her early 40s who came to see me for depression. Sara's parents, like many parents of her generation, expressed their love in a practical way – providing clean clothes, food on the table, fussing over manners, asking if she's done her homework, etc. They also had four children to contend with. So Sara recalled growing up rather 'starved' of overt demonstrations of affection and developed a keen sensitivity to feeling 'rejection'. Sara ended up being very overweight, not untypical with many clients 'starved' of affection. A year prior to our sessions, Sara had participated in a dieting programme and lost six stones in weight. While she personally felt delighted, fitter and more energetic and attractive, she faced a mixed reception to her success. Her previously friendly female boss, who was also overweight, now spoke to her in a rather brusque and curt fashion. On another occasion, Sara was at a picnic with some friends when the husband of one of her female friends (who had himself lost a lot of weight in a dieting regime), commented on Sara's progress and how much better she looked. From then on Sara received a frosty reception from the man's wife.

Sara's inner advocate panicked at the thought of rejection and immediately sought to appease and placate these other people who were in some way offended by Sara's increased attractiveness. So Sara put all the weight she lost back on, plus some extra for good measure. No wonder Sara came in feeling depressed. Her emotional self had been looked after and she had been feeling healthier and more attractive, then these experiences were snatched away on the grounds that it made others jealous. The inner child could not help responding in turn with the feeling of: 'Okay, so the message is that everyone else's needs are more important than mine and I'm not allowed to be happy if others don't approve!' which would make any child feel depressed. Understandably it was sad because her inner advocate, rather than supporting her, had forgotten who its client was and who it was meant to

> be representing. Instead, it acted as if other people were its clients. Training herself to realise who the main priority was helped Sara lift her depression and get back to losing weight and looking after herself.

As a general rule-of-thumb – if you, as the acting advocate, allow your client to end up in a situation where terms are being dictated to him or her, then you will have failed in your duty. You have allowed your client to be put in a 'victim' position where his or her feelings and preferences are not being taken into account. Your client absolutely detests being placed in any kind of victim or 'one-down' position because of your failure to fight for his or her needs and will blame and resent you any time it feels you haven't done your job properly.

Conversely, you will know when you have done your job when, instead, your client is able to choose from a range of options, because choice means your client is not being forced into anything but has is able to act from a place of autonomy and free will, which is an incredibly important value for it. On this note, a useful tip is the 'three-choices' response.

Someone once said, in *any* situation, you always have three choices:

1. To *do* what is asked.
2. To *not do* what is asked.
3. To do something *completely different*.

So as an advocate, always look for three choices for your client in any given situation and that's when you will know you have done your job and got true choice for your client. It does not even matter if you end up agreeing to do choice number 1 (to do what was asked) as long as you have been given the freedom to reflect on all the options present, evaluate your best interests and then choose the best course of action for you, which happens to be option 1. It would still be in alignment with your free will.

For example: imagine that your workplace is fast becoming a toxic environment because your new boss is a real tyrant. Your boss is on some kind of power trip and starts treating the staff as they were his slaves, which is offending your sense of pride and dignity.

An inner consultation process between your inner advocate and inner child might go something like:

INNER CHILD: Upset, upset, upset...

INNER ADULT: [starting with validation and clarification mode] What kind of 'upset' is that?

INNER CHILD: It's my boss. I'm beginning to really dislike working there and that smug expression that shows he thinks he 'owns' us.

INNER ADULT: [now that the need has been identified activates advocate role] Okay, Felix, we have at least three options. We could give the boss a piece of our mind and quit. We could humour him while we look for another job. Or we could do something different such as save up and go travelling. Which do you prefer? If you feel very strongly about it, I will pursue option number one for you.

INNER CHILD: Hmm, even though I often feel like giving the boss a piece of my mind, it is not convenient for me to quit right now. I might lose the deposit on my flat if I can't pay the rent any more and why should I allow my life to be inconvenienced by my boss? So I *choose* not to have this inconvenience right now. Instead, I choose to give it three more months, then look for another job. If I can't find another job right then, I'll have saved some money to quit and take a break.

INNER ADULT: Okay, if that's what you want.

However, what if your boss is actually on the whole a nice guy, but there are other problems to contend with that need less drastic solutions? How might the inner advocate handle these? Here's another example:

INNER CHILD: Upset, upset, upset...

INNER ADULT: What kind of 'upset' is that?

INNER CHILD: The upset is from work. As I was leaving, the boss took me aside and said, 'Felix, can you do me a favour – because you're such a nice guy and helpful... Could you edit these reports for me? I know it's technically Gavin's job, but you know how difficult it is getting Gavin to do anything round here. But you're a nice guy, so could you do it?' Initially I accepted because I like being flattered, thinking it was just twenty minutes' work, but when I got home I realised I got myself into four hours' work and now I'm going to have to sacrifice a large part of my valuable free time...

INNER ADULT: [now that the need has been identified

activates advocate role] Okay, well, that constitutes taking liberties, so I'm going to politely return this work to him.

The inner advocate is clear about his job brief: to establish boundaries between acceptable and unacceptable work. The next day:

> INNER ADVOCATE: Boss, can we speak for a moment? You know yesterday you asked me to do that work and I said yes ... well, in hindsight, it's much more work than I expected. I already have a full workload of my own, so I'm really sorry but I'm going to have to return it to you.
> FELIX'S BOSS: Oh, c'mon, Felix, you know how difficult and unreliable Gavin can be and getting him to do anything causes a massive headache...

The advocate is not swayed. He reminds himself: 'Who is my client here? It's not Gavin, it's not my boss, it's Felix, so it's his interests I need to uphold.' (It's a lot easier to defend boundaries when you know which ones you have to defend.)

> INNER ADVOCATE: 'Boss, I do sympathise, but I have my own problems and Gavin's issues are not my problem. Either train him, discipline him, transfer or fire him, but I am not responsible for Gavin's attitude to work.'

If the boss is decent, he will generally respect your boundaries. If he is not, you also have a choice as to whether you want to work for that kind of person or look for another job.

Acting as an advocate is not about being confrontational, antagonistic or other people. It's about respecting your needs as well as those of others and being firm when needed. It means knowing your 'bottom line' agenda for yourself and politely but firmly sticking to that in the face of other people trying to impose their agenda on you. My favourite polite but firm phrases are 'I'm sorry, but...' and 'I sympathise, but...' Obviously if politeness does not work, by all means let your inner advocate let rip if that's the only thing that will get through, but that should be a last port of call.

Note that the inner advocate aspect is not a passive role that's merely there to obey the wishes of the client without question. It's a proactive leadership role of advising the client about what their best interests might be, which might require occasionally challenging their immediate wishes in order to gain an even bigger, long-term benefit down the line.

Let's imagine one more variable was present in our last example, in which case the advocate would act as follows:

INNER ADVOCATE: Okay, Felix, if you feel really strongly, I'll take this work back. But I'd like you to consider that we have a new position coming up in the company and it could really help us if we had the boss on our side. So what would you prefer to do?

INNER CHILD: Hmm ... I do want that promotion, so I guess I could sacrifice one evening to be owed a favour.

INNER ADVOCATE: Okay, leave to me, I'll arrange it.

The next day:

INNER ADVOCATE: Boss, can we speak for a moment? You know the other day you asked me to do that work and I said yes ... Look, it is more work than I originally thought when I accepted, but I will do it for you in return for a favour. Could you put in a good word for me in the application for this new position?

Here the advocate is still fulfilling the principles of negotiating for the ultimate best deal for his client.

The inner advocate in the private domain

The advocate 'hat' is not just for work and one's professional life, but also needs to be worn in our private lives. Let's say I arrive home quite tired and receive a call from my friend Steve.

> STEVE: Felix, there's a Paris Hilton film festival in the local cinema. I'm a great fan of hers, so please drop everything and come with me.
> INNER ADVOCATE: [In the past I would have said, 'Okay, Steve, I'll be there,' in the misguided notion of friends always help their friends, regardless. Instead, now with my advocate hat on, I 'check with my client' first] Felix, what is it you really want to do tonight?
> INNER CHILD: You know, I'm really tired and I was hoping to just rest, chill out, have a good soak in the bath with a glass of wine and listen to some music this evening.
> INNER ADVOCATE: Well, if that's your 'brief', then leave it to me.
> INNER ADVOCATE [to Steve]: Steve, you know Paris Hilton films are really not my cup of tea and I've kind of made plans tonight to rest and catch up on my sleep. But you have a great time and we'll catch up some other time.

STEVE: Come on, Felix, no one else will come to see the
Paris Hilton festival with me. I'll have to go alone.

INNER ADVOCATE: Well, Steve, I guess you can either go
alone, wait for the DVD or join the Paris Hilton fan club
and meet other kindred spirits. Sorry, but I can't go
against the wishes of my client.

Steve realises that he will not be able to impose his inner
child's agenda over mine. This also teaches Steve to respect
my agenda more in the future.

As with the earlier example with the professional domain
and the advocate advising me to take the work my boss
asked me to do in return for being owed an important
favour, the advocate also proactively urges me to take any
action that would benefit me in the long run in the private
domain as well.

Imagine for a moment that my friend Steve invited me to
a different outing:

STEVE: Felix, there's a party on tonight. C'mon, drop everything. Let's go.

INNER ADVOCATE: [consults with inner child] Felix, what is
it you want to do tonight?

INNER CHILD: Ah, I don't know. I can't really be bothered.
I'd rather veg out at home and watch *Friends*.

INNER ADVOCATE: [sensing this is not a bona fide case of
needing rest but sounds more like lethargy or laziness]
Hmm, well, on a scale of one to ten, how tired are you
truthfully?

INNER CHILD: About a four.

INNER ADVOCATE: Well, if you said seven or above, I would

happily put my foot down, but four sounds like a case of lethargy and inertia. So, c'mon, just stick on a T-shirt and some jeans, you'll catch your second wind in the process. You're still young. Go on, enjoy life a bit. Reruns of *Friends* are always on.

INNER ADVOCATE: [after the party] So, did you have a good time?

INNER CHILD: Yeah, I had a blast, glad I went.

INNER ADVOCATE: You see, that's why I make a point of remembering the things you like so that next time something like this occurs I'll say, 'Remember the last time you didn't want to go to a party, but you went in the end and you were really grateful that you did? C'mon, accept this invitation too.'

How might your inner child feel to have a healthy inner advocate in their camp? Float into the inner child position and imagine for several months you have been witnessing your inner adult defending your best interests and fighting your corner for a change, continuing to back up words with action. If you feel that someone is fighting for you, it must mean they care for you enough to do so, that you are worth fighting for. To fight for someone involves respecting them and respecting their needs. You begin to feel more worthy of respect. As your adult continues to fight to protect or pursue your needs, you begin to trust that your adult has upgraded your importance and is making you more of a priority than a doormat who will put up with anything. Your assertiveness and self-respect will increase.

Step 8: Be your own reality checker

Your inner child or emotional self reacts 'emotionally' to things. That is, it tends to take things personally and it tends to 'catastrophise' about the outcomes (a negative global generalisation such as 'this has ruined my life for ever' or 'no one will ever want to go out with me again'). It is a child after all and just its nature to process information that way. However, if left unchecked, these emotional reactions could just feed in on themselves leading to even more distorted and warped views about reality, which could lead to anxiety and depression.

Do you remember the first crush you ever had? It could be towards a person your age, a neighbour, a celebrity, pop star, movie star or anyone. If so, for a while you were besotted with the object of your affection and could think of no one else. I remember dating a girl once who had such a crush on the actor George Clooney that you could literally talk about algebra and somehow George Clooney's name would enter the conversation.

Then of course, your crush may have waned and you got bored with the object of your desire and found a new person to lavish your attention on. What about the first person you had a crush on? What about all the heartfelt proclamations of 'I can't imagine a life without them'? What happened to all these vows? At the time the inner child was in the throes of one if its generalisations. It confused feeling strongly about someone or something in that *moment* with feeling that way for *all* time. If it feels sad with the end of a relationship, it feels as if it will feel this way for the rest of its life ('I will never get over this'). Then it will become anxious or despairing at being trapped at feeling pain for the rest of its life. And it doesn't seem to learn. Never mind that it may have repeated this same pattern – saying the same things, feeling the same 'everlasting' feelings, the same never-ending despair and hopelessness – half a dozen times or more with many different crushes or relationships. It may go on doing the same thing over and over again indefinitely unless it has some kind of moderating influence or reality-checking done by the inner adult.

The inner adult's job is to gently challenge the emotional overreactions and generalisations of the inner child with a reality check: 'I know you feel that way but you've said this a dozen times before in the past and you always get over it, you always move on or find someone or something new. I know it seems like the end of the world at the moment, but remember that you are just going through a phase, nothing stays the same for ever and all things change. Have hope that things can work out and you will be find things to take pleasure in again. That's what you've already done many times before.'

So if you find yourself taking things personally and always expect the worst-case scenario, this means that any reality checks provided by your inner adult mind during those times have failed to have an effect. Why might this be? Perhaps the inner adult does not know how to offer a helpful reality check, but more often than not, it's because of the *way* the conscious mind tries to check reality, rather than the actual logic behind its argument. Reality checks in the form of 'don't be silly' or 'it won't kill you' will invalidate and alienate the inner child, causing it to clam up and stop listening to anything else you say, no matter how sensible. The trick is take the feelings of the inner child seriously, without actually taking the problem seriously and reading more into it than there is.

EXAMPLE OF A REALITY CHECK

INNER CHILD: [distress call] Upset, upset.

INNER ADULT: [starting with clarification and validation] Okay, what kind of 'upset' is that? Is it anger, sadness, fear, hurt ...?

INNER CHILD: I'm anxious because of the bust-up I had with my best friend, Sally. I got really mad and told her I never want to see her again and I can't believe I've just lost my best friend for ever and I'll never find anyone like her ever again, oh woe is me, what's wrong with me, why do I always...

INNER ADULT: [validating the experience] Okay, I know you feel upset right now because you feel you've lost your best friend for ever and it must feel so awful for you right now, but you know, the flip side of love can often be intense, passionate fallouts and good friends often experience this not just once, but several times in the course of a close relationship.

[INNER ADULT considers this new way of interpreting the experience.]

INNER ADULT: [continues] ...and you know what, I bet you Sally feels the same way as you. She doesn't want to lose this friendship, which you both value, so this is what I'll do to resolve the situation. I'll take the initiative and call Sally and offer her an olive branch of peace.

INNER CHILD: What if she doesn't accept it and wants to stay mad for ever?

INNER ADULT: Well, I really doubt she will feel that way if she's your real friend, but this bad blood will definitely continue if no one does anything. Trust me and I bet you I'm right about this.

[INNER ADULT telephones Sally.]

INNER ADULT: Hi, Sally, look I really didn't mean the things I said the other day. I was really out of line, so I'm really sorry. I don't want to lose you as my best friend.

Now that everyone has calmed down, it's probable that Sally is also feeling contrite and sheepish and wants to make things better again too. Sally is likely to say, 'Well, I'm sorry too. I said some mean things and was out of line.' Pretty soon we are both apologising to each other and confessing that our meanness caused the other to react uncharacteristically. All the while the subconscious mind is observing the conscious mind's advice has paid off and is worth trusting.

Here's another example of a reality check in terms of finding an appropriate sense of control.

INNER CHILD: [distress call] Upset, upset.

INNER ADULT: [starting with clarification and validation] Okay, what kind of 'upset' is that?

INNER CHILD: Well, I've got my French A-levels soon and I'm worried that if I don't do well my life will be over … All my friends will go to France while I have to do my retakes, I won't go to the university I want and all my friends will go to another, then I'll be miserable and won't study so I won't get my degree, so I'll end up without any qualifications and sweep roads for the rest of my life and then my life will be over ...

INNER ADULT: Okay, hold on, I know you feel like your life depends on this exam and if you don't do well you will be miserable for ever and so you want to control the future to make it safe, but let's just pause and take stock of things for a moment. The only thing you need to control right now is just doing the best you can for that exam and that's it. You know, even if you have a head-ache or a cold or a really tricky question that comes up every few years, that's unfortunate but it happens. It has to happen to someone and that includes us. Even if these unlucky things turn up, your job remains to just do the best you can with it and see what happens next. Whatever happens, we will work it out. If we need to retake exams, we'll retake them.

If you feel strongly about your French comprehen-sion, I will get you some extra tuition for any areas you want extra practice on, but do you really need it or are you just having a worrying moment?

INNER CHILD: No, I know everything. I was just worried about what would happen in the future, but now I remember to just focus on delivering my best effort on the day and that's it. That's the only thing I am respon-sible for. The rest is not in my control and for me to worry about.

For the inner child, going from being told to 'stop being silly' to having your inner adult calmly listening, accepting your feelings and also leading you to a useful alternative outcome, must be a very nice change. It helps to make the inner child more secure and trusting that things can be taken care of, rather than being worried to death about them. Feeling more secure and trusting 'oneself' more will also enhance confidence.

Step 9: Be a great problem-solver

In one sense life can be thought of as a series of problems needing solutions. So for a child to prosper in life, its parents need to teach it how to be good at solving problems. The better children become at solving problems, the less anxious they will feel, the more confident they will become and the more they will flourish.

Problem-solving and troubleshooting is a big field and does depend on the context, but here are just a few of the important elements involved.

1. Creating viable response plans

If you are faced with a challenge but are armed with a trusty viable plan to navigate your way through that challenge, then already a lot of your anxiety and uncertainty can be laid to rest because it's almost as if you have a map telling you what to do or where to go next, to see you through this territory until you reach safe ground again.

Here's an example of a viable plan in action from my past:

Viable plan: The incident with Neville

Here's the background to this problem: I rent out consulting rooms in my clinic and I have very laid-back and generous terms of usage compared to many other rental arrangements out there. For instance, most renters would need to pay rent in advance, have a fixed number of hours, pay during their holidays, etc. In contrast, therapists using my rooms pay only for the hours they use and have until the end of the following month to settle an invoice. The only thing I need to be a bit of a stickler about is that when payments are due, they are made on time because I need rent in by certain dates to pay several banking standing orders, otherwise there's a risk of going overdrawn.

Many years ago I rented a consulting room to a person I'll call Neville. When the due date for me receiving his rent had expired by a few days, I sent him a polite email reminding him that rent was due and, given the already generous terms of paying after the rentals rather than in advance, punctual payment really was a necessary requirement. A few days later, I saw that Neville had made an electronic payment to my bank account, without an accompanying email offering any sort of admission of lateness or apology. 'Never mind,' I thought. 'People are busy, maybe he didn't have time, but at least now we've sorted that out.' When payment was next due for the second month, again the expiry period had come and gone and once again I did not receive payment in time. I sent Neville another polite email reminder and, as before, I received electronic payment a few days later without so much as a 'sorry' for the lateness, despite the terms and conditions of rental now being twice overlooked. Again, I reasoned that perhaps Neville was very busy (I knew he had several children) or that my message had not sunk in yet or perhaps organisation was not his strong point, but that eventually my few terms of rental would be adhered to. Halfway through his third month of usage, Neville announced that he would no longer commute to London for work and would concentrate on finding therapy rooms in his hometown, so he would not be booking any more rooms after the end of the week. My patient had just arrived, so I wished Neville luck and assumed that he would probably leave a cheque in my pigeonhole to settle for his hours so far that month. At the end of the evening, I noticed that he had not left any form of payment, so I reasoned that technically he was still entitled to hold off until the due date in six weeks' time. Perhaps he was short of funds, so I would wait until that time. The last date for payment came and went. I waited an additional extra few days and still nothing. That night, there was an internal 'niggle' that prevented me going to sleep. Since I'm usually a good sleeper, I know enough about my subconscious mind to understand that any internal nagging is mostly just my emotional self being concerned about something and wanting reassurance that it will be dealt with. The inner child hates problems that are 'live' without some sort of action plan assigned to them to address them. So here's what I had to do:

INNER CHILD: Upset, upset!

INNER ADULT: Okay, what kind of upset is that?

INNER CHILD: It's that bloody Neville. He really ticks me off. He's already benefiting from these generous terms and all I ask for is one concession to punctuality and he ignores it. He's taking liberties and what if he thinks he can get away with not paying me? I don't trust him to even pay any more, since he seems so reluctant to part with his money unless I keep pestering him…

INNER ADULT: [starting with validation] Okay, so you're understandably upset about this person not seeming to respect your generous business relationship and angry at the idea that he might try to renege on his final payment?

INNER CHILD: Yes, I mean, how dare he? I should…

INNER ADULT: Okay, hold on… no one is running off with our money because you're so upset that your forgetting the 'system' I have in place for such contingencies.

INNER CHILD: Huh?

INNER ADULT: Well, step one of the 'system' is I send

Neville a polite email stating: 'Dear Neville, according to my records, I don't seem to have received your payment yet, which is now overdue as per the agreed terms and conditions. Please pay ASAP.'

INNER CHILD: So? He'll probably just ignore that as well.

INNER ADULT: Yes, but then that leads to step two, which is a second email one week later that goes: 'Dear Neville, further to my previous email, with regret, unless I receive payment within one week, I will have to pass the matter over to my debt-collection agency, which will involve an additional admin fee of £50.00 plus any additional costs.' Now, we don't have to worry whether Neville will honour his side of the contract out of morality and fairness because were relying on his sense of self-interest. If he's so reluctant to part with his money, the last thing he wants is to lose £50 needlessly. I have proof that he used the rooms, so if it came to any kind of court hearing, he knows he would lose and pay costs, so he'd be crazy to go there. The worst-case scenario is not that we won't get the money owed back but that we will be slightly inconvenienced and delayed for a couple of weeks.

INNER CHILD: [can see why this plan would work, feels more secure now knowing a resolution is in hand, so is ready to go back to sleep undisturbed]

INNER ADULT: [adding a bit of reality checking]: Besides,

one of the things about being self-employed is there's no accounts department to deal with these hassles, but, if these things really annoy you, do you want to work for someone else and have another of their departments deal with these things?

INNER CHILD: No, I really like all the benefits of being self-employed.

INNER ADULT: Well, then this is what goes with that territory. Also if you think about it, what's the real damage of these kinds of delayed payments anyway? They're nothing more than a bit of a nuisance and inconvenience that need only a bit of time sending a few emails and that's a very minor price for being self-employed, isn't it?

My inner child felt that this concern was addressed by having faith in the viable plan proposed, so it could turn off its 'alarm' status and allow me to go to sleep.

And yes, Neville did eventually pay up.

2. Solving problems via mediation

You've doubtless had the experience of having two people close to you argue with each other. Since you care about the needs of both people arguing, but you're not personally involved in the argument itself, you're in a neutral position where you are able to see the relative merits of each person's point of view, whereas they have become bogged down with miscommunications and misunderstandings of each other's points.

Perhaps you calmly intervened to help return their attention to the points of the argument that were being overlooked and then pointed them to some kind of obvious, practical solution that they couldn't see because they were caught up in the emotions of the argument. If so, you have mediated a conflict between two sides. Needless to say, there is a need to mediate between the different agendas and needs of the inner adult and inner child, especially when the relationship between them can be characterised as a kind of endlessly bickering couple. This is where the input of the inner grandparent becomes especially valuable and where a more active role is forthcoming.

Here's an example of the inner grandparents mediating between the two minds:

INNER ADULT: [focusing only on his adult agenda]: Right, let's see, I have six free hours today. I can use that time to do all my accounts and invoices.

INNER CHILD: Oh God, not the whole day! All we ever do is work and no play. It's sunny and I want to go for a walk today.

INNER ADULT: No time, walking is frivolous – I need to do my accounts. So, I'll start with my backlog of VAT, then I'll do my invoices, then...

INNER CHILD: [sending strong avoidant feelings] I don't want to do that work today.

Six hours later

INNER ADULT: 'I don't understand why I've had six hours to do my accounts and I still haven't done them. I've even had a strong desire to do work, but somehow this desire ended up with me doing non-urgent work like cleaning all my windows, rather than accounts. I just don't get it. Well, today is another write-off, but at least I can spend the whole of tomorrow doing my accounts again!

INNER CHILD: He's still not getting the message! Obviously I need to make it louder – avoid accounts, avoid accounts, avoid accounts!

INNER GRANDPARENT: [sees the problem situation and calmly intervenes] Okay, you two have been having a really unproductive conflict about your priorities where you both end up having the worst of both worlds. So, inner child, let's start with you, what is it you wanted to have happened today?

INNER CHILD: Well, I really need to go for a walk and enjoy the autumn scenery before it all goes and I'm bored with being cooped up in the office all day.

INNER GRANDPARENT: Okay and what about you, the adult?

INNER ADULT: Well, as long as I do my last month's accounts, I'm happy. I can do the rest later on.

INNER GRANDPARENT: And how long will it take for you to do those accounts?

INNER ADULT: [thinks about it] Three hours if I really focus.

INNER GRANDPARENT: Okay, let's make that the goal. So how are you both with this: tomorrow we work for three hours until 2 p.m., then no matter where you're at, we go for a walk in the park?

INNER CHILD: Yes, as long as I get to go the park, I'm happy

and I won't interfere in conscious mind's business beforehand because I know I get my walk in the sunshine.

INNER ADULT: And if I finish off last month's invoices, that's
a good day's work, so I won't drag my heels either when
it's time to go to the park.

INNER GRANDPARENT: Good, so we are all agreed.

In my own experience, I've seen that whenever I've taken
the time to weigh up the different needs of different parts
of me and made a plan to include all of them, I've had the
most productive day, felt more in control, more certain and
with the added bonus of increased productivity as less
energy is wasted through avoidance and procrastination.
It's a win–win situation – everyone is happy because they
feel their needs have been respected and listened to, and
there is no need to be competitive and obstruct the agenda
of other parts.

What might be the effect upon your inner child of being
shown how to solve problems in a constructive way? Well,
float into the inner-child part and have a virtual experience
to see for yourself. Imagine coming across a new problem.
You start off feeling uncertain about how to proceed and
uncertainty makes you apprehensive and insecure because
you don't know what is involved in solving this problem.
The problem facing you could be a 'mountain' to overcome
or merely a molehill. To play it safe, your instincts opt for
the worst-case scenario and prepare for a long struggle. A
mountain of effort to overcome sounds tedious, laborious
and boring. In other words, it sounds like a mountain of
'pain' and your instincts are designed to spare you from
pain by avoiding it. Then your inner adult steps into the

fray, wearing its problem-solving hat. Your inner adult calmly reminds you that although problems tend to look like mountains at first, if you stay with the problem a little longer and get to know it better, the mountain begins to shrink.

The inner adult instructs you into a simple plan for dealing with 'mountains', which is, rather than trying to tackle the whole thing at once and feel overwhelmed, start to break the mountain up into little molehills or small 'digestible' component parts. Then decide which component you need to attend to first, then second, then third – and then that's enough for one day. Tomorrow, pick up from where you left off until all the components are dealt with. The inner adult could add a helpful analogy such as: if you're not scared by doing a ten-piece jigsaw puzzle in ten minutes, then it makes no difference whether you spend ten minutes every day for a couple of years doing a *new* ten-piece mini jigsaw puzzle or spend ten minutes every day for a couple of years working on ten pieces of an *ongoing* 10,000-piece jigsaw. It's exactly the same work; the only difference is the interpretation of how much effort is needed.

After the problem is resolved, your inner adult will continue to remind you of your past successes when you encounter other problems in the future. Your adult draws your attention back to the bigger picture – that problems will initially always look scarier than they are and although you feel like fleeing, just remember you do have the power to convert mountains into molehills. Once you've had that assurance, you will invariably end up feeling 'That was easy, why didn't I do it sooner? Must remember next time.'

And so your confidence and faith in your abilities to solve problems grows and grows so you no longer avoid them or are put off by them. Which means you become more secure in your abilities and have more trust and faith in yourself to pull through tough times.

On other occasions, the inner grandparent steps in to help mediate between your needs and those of the other necessary needs of the inner adult, until you are satisfied that your agenda is respected.

These new approaches must make a nice change from the inner adult's previous approaches to your problems, which was to fob you off, ignore or criticise you. This undermined your confidence, as well as kept the original problem 'live' (which means you couldn't switch off and feel it was going to be addressed, so you always carried around a background anxiety).

When a child is free to be a child, it can be more true to its real nature, which is to be playful, creative, spontaneous and fun. If you've ever been around real children in this way, this fun is infectious and pretty soon us serious adults are on the floor playing games and being charmed. In my consulting rooms, whenever people tell me that they are no longer having any 'fun' in their lives, I see the situation as a chronically neglected inner child who has been overlooked in the service of the almighty adult to-do list. The tyranny of the to-do list causes the inner child in us to retreat, and fun, spontaneity and creativity tend to retreat with it. Make time for that side of you because it is there. Check in and see what that side of you wants and then you will start to feel the playfulness and fun returning to your life.

Step 10: Discipline with love

As a parent you are in a position of authority and power over another person, and with great power comes great responsibility. Children are programmed to pursue pleasure and avoid what they see as pain. They live in the moment, they don't always know when they have had enough of a good thing (e.g. eating sweets until they feel sick), they avoid things that they would actually like if they allowed themselves to experience them and they have trouble seeing the bigger picture (such as foregoing immediate gratification for greater longer-term benefits in the future). It is your job to apply appropriate discipline to establish necessary boundaries to steer them towards healthy paths that they cannot yet appreciate and to endure the necessary resistance, resentment, defiance, ungratefulness or any other uncooperative behaviour on the way. Why do you put up with trying to help someone and receiving abuse back? Because you love them and have their best interests at heart. You want what is right for them, even if it makes you the bad guy in their eyes at that time. Being a parent should not be a popularity contest, it's about doing your duty to your child. Not just the nice bits but the unpleasant bits too.

In this sense, the parenting job entails a level of professionalism similar to that in the working world. A true 'professional' does not let personal issues interfere with their job. They do their job regardless of how tired they are, whatever else is going on in their life or how they feel about their clients and they don't take other people's upsets personally. Professionals focus on a higher calling, perhaps on the value they place on doing a job well and professionally. In a parent's case, as mentioned above, it's about the welfare of their child.

Discipline is the tool the adult uses to move the child towards those necessary things that they'd otherwise avoid, however hard that might be on the parent, and love is the driving force that fuels the parent to apply this discipline, regardless of how difficult it might seem.

Being a 'professional' parent

We've all had experiences of people who are professional and unprofessional in their jobs. Not only is so much nicer to be on the receiving end of professional service or conduct, it's also nicer for the professional themselves. Professionals enjoy their jobs more because there is a real pleasure in knowing one is good at one's job. Others also notice this and may provide positive feedback. Consequently, professionals esteem and value their jobs and therefore themselves more, because they acknowledge that they are good at doing jobs that they value.

In this sense, as your inner adult carries out his or her parenting job and does it with a similar sense of professional pride, you will also gain a personal boost of achievement that comes from knowing that you are doing your job well.

Unprofessional parenting

What prevents the inner adult from acting in such a desired professional manner? Some of the main reasons have already been covered – the inner adult judging the inner child, which stifles empathy and blames the inner child for being deliberately difficult and resistant.

In this segment there are three additional reasons that prevent good parenting: lazy parenting, confusing parental needs with the child's needs and running a popularity contest.

LAZY PARENTING

Imagine a dialogue between a parent who is a wealthy businessman and their teenage son or daughter.

TEENAGER: It's my 16th birthday, perhaps we can all go out and spend time together to celebrate.

PARENT: [too busy thinking of his job in the City] No time for that, I'll make it up to you but Daddy loves you. Look here's a sports car instead.

TEENAGER: [thinking] Why can't he even spend time with me instead of work? It's not like he ever needs to work again anyway. I won't be bought off with consumer goods instead of quality time and attention. I guess I just must not be important enough for him to want to spend time with me.

A few weeks later

PARENT: I don't understand why my son has crashed the car under the influence. Why is he so unhappy? I've given him everything. Well, I'll get him into the best rehab and get him the best medical help possible because I love him and would do anything for him.

In this case the father has provided every material need and thought he was being a great parent by just lavishing money on the child. That is sloppy and lazy parenting. A parent needs to consider the impact of their actions on the child and plan accordingly. It's fine to lavish gifts on your children if you also exercise due discipline in the process, so that you teach them how to value and respect things, rather than spoiling them and allowing them to take things for granted.

If your inner adult thinks that throwing money at the inner child is an acceptable substitute for spending any real quality time or attention, then it's time to re-evaluate the situation. Your inner child might either lose all interest in material goods and feel something is missing or it might mistakenly confuse money with love and keep pushing you to demonstrate that you love him or her by buying bigger and better things to fill that love gap, which just never seems to be filled.

CONFUSING PARENTAL NEEDS WITH THE CHILD'S NEEDS

I've often heard parents say things such as, 'I still insist my 18-year-old daughter comes back at 10 p.m. or cannot go out alone. I just love her too much.' I've also heard some parents proudly state: 'I couldn't possibly allow my daughter to study in America for three years, I love her too much', as if not being able to bear being parted from her daughter's company is the highest manifestation of real love.

What effect do such statements have on the daughter? It confuses her. The daughter resents the fact that her preferences are overridden, but she then feels guilty because it was claimed that her preferences were vetoed in the name of love.

How can she blame her parents for loving her too much? After all, isn't getting love the main goal of any child? But whose needs are actually being served here: the child's or the parents'? Her parents are sincere in their belief that their behaviour is loving behaviour, but that doesn't mean it is. The real message is: 'I can't bear my own anxiety or loneliness when you are gone, so please can you change your plans accordingly so I don't suffer.' Instead, a more loving response would be: 'If that's what you really want to do to make you fulfilled, I'll miss you, but go with my blessing.' Inside the parent might be feeling, 'God, I'll miss you so much', but it would be unfair to use that as a guilt trip to influence the daughter's decision. The parent needs to set her free to do that and bear the pain of the distance.

A loving response for the other example might be: 'Well, Jane knows to only get licensed black cabs and to always travel with a friend and avoid any threatening areas so there's no real reason to impose an inappropriate curfew time for her age and intelligence. She knows how to take suitable action to protect herself when she goes out. Personally, I won't rest until I hear her come back in, but that's my problem not hers.'

As the inner adult, I recommend you begin to question some of your own cherished notions. For instance, if you work too much ('for the sake of the child'), then think about your real motives. Does your inner child actually want you to work that much? Are you really doing it for him or her or is work a place where you enjoy the status you have, where you feel more familiar and in control, where you feel more important, flattered and no one questions your decisions? If so, it's important to be honest and accept these things. They can be worked through, but your inner child needs to trust you and it needs to feel you are being honest with it, rather than meeting your needs while claiming that you are doing it on its behalf.

PUTTING POPULARITY FIRST

Consider another imaginary dialogue between a mother and her teenage daughter.

> MOTHER: [wanting to be liked and seen as young and hip]
>   Let's be best friends, go double-dating and share sex tips
>   and be just like two sisters.
> DAUGHTER: [mixed feelings, thinks] Part of me is flattered
>   by this special attention and closeness that my friends
>   don't have with their mother. But the rest of me feels
>   uneasy about this. I want a mother so I can be a
>   daughter.

The daughter wants to be told off when she has crossed a line rather than be pandered to and she is being cheated of her lessons about boundaries and appropriate conduct. Her lessons are being hijacked by the mother's more urgent need to feel young or feel popular. The daughter correctly senses that this is more about the mother than about her own needs.

As an inner adult to yourself, remember that seeking popularity above the needs of the child is irresponsible and uncaring behaviour. It's as if you would be taking out huge loans to pamper the child to court her popularity that she will end up having to pay down the line and which will make her go into debt. Ironically, doing the right thing will make you more popular in the long term.

Discipline with love in action

As you face your inner child across from you clamouring for something or other, rather than rushing in to appease it to get it off your back, take a moment to prepare yourself. Put on your metaphorical 'professional' hat. This focuses your intent on your true job at hand. It reminds you to focus on the best interests of your client, even when they cannot understand or appreciate them, and to not let your own personal stuff get in the way.

Secondly, ask yourself, 'What does my inner child need to learn here? What's the bigger picture that would benefit his or her long-term development?' Having clarified the best course of action, stick to your purpose and the boundaries you need to establish. You remain clear about what is needed and why it is important. You already expect and accept that your inner child will push all the boundaries on principle, to resist anything that is not immediate gratification. But as a professional you don't take it personally. While it may be tough, knowing this helps you to maintain your professional composure. Then you are ready to address the child's wants:

INNER CHILD: Upset, upset!

INNER ADULT: What kind of 'upset' is that?

INNER CHILD: Want a bar of chocolate.

INNER ADULT: Okay, well, kids do like chocolate. You haven't had a treat in a while, so one bar will be okay. [buys a chocolate bar]

INNER CHILD: [wolfs down chocolate] Want another.

INNER ADULT: Hold on, you asked for one bar and I got one as a treat, but two bars is getting into unhealthy eating habits. I'm responsible for your health and it's bad for your health to make this a habit, so if you are still hungry I'd gladly get you some fruit.

INNER CHILD: Don't care, want chocolate.

INNER ADULT: 'Repeat, one bar is a treat; two is bad. If you're hungry, I'll get you some fruit.

INNER CHILD: [using cunning and manipulation] I thought you liked me and would do anything for me?

INNER ADULT: I do. That's why I'm doing the best thing for you here.

INNER CHILD: [persisting] John's dad buys John all the chocolates John wants. John's dad must really love John. I wish you were like John's dad. He's nice to his son.

INNER ADULT: [not taking the bait] Be that as it may, John's dad can do whatever he wants with his son, no matter how irresponsible, but you are my responsibility and two bars is irresponsible. I repeat – no more chocolate, but I will happily get you some fruit instead.

It can seem to be a contest of wills and in any contest you as the parent need to show you have more endurance and patience; in short, that you are stronger than the child. If you cave in, the child will learn to walk over you and will take away the lesson that the way to get their needs met is by having tantrums or by nagging or manipulating others, which would be setting it up for a lot of problems in relationships in the future.

Now float into the inner child and experience what it's

like to receive discipline with love. You've just been given a bar of chocolate but you wanted more and your adult firmly said 'no'. Even though on the surface you may be fuming, resentful, hurt or angry, deep down you are secretly delighted. You figure: 'Wow, will you look at that? He or she is willing to risk being unpopular and hated to do what's right for me. So this really is about me, not about him. He must truly care for me. THAT is love!'

The child will respect and trust you more down the line because it knows you always act in its best interest.

You can see that by applying the principle of loving discipline, one can be a kind, generous and loving adult without ending up spoiling the child.

Taking stock of self-parenting

So, let's take stock of the effect of the sum total of all these ten principles of self-parenting on you.

Imagine that it is a good three months down the line and you have been consistently practising all these principles on yourself.

Firstly, float into the inner adult perspective, facing the inner child and:

- Notice what kind of relationship you are having now with your inner child.
- How do you feel now about him or her and about yourself in contrast to before?
- Notice how much clearer, knowledgeable and effective you have become as a manager. Notice how you are

refining your powers of discernment and making appropriate decisions based on the merits of each case, rather than employing a one-size-fits-all approach.

- Notice how, over time, you have earned the trust and respect of your inner child as a result of your increasing effectiveness as its parent.
- Notice how this has raised your self-esteem and your inner belief in your ability and capacity to accomplish your tasks.

Now float out of the inner child and look back at your inner adult and take stock of what it feels like to be parented in the new way.

Because actions speak louder than words, your adult has been putting their money where their mouth is, which means you have increasingly grown to trust him or her more over time. You are growing in faith and confidence in your adult's ability to care and look after you, so you feel more secure and in safe hands.

- Notice what kind of relationship you are having now with your inner adult. You probably feel more cherished, attended to, secure, protected, validated, acknowledged, understood, accepted, tutored, coached, praised and esteemed in general.
- How do you feel now about your inner adult and about yourself in contrast to before?

The way you feel about yourself depends on how you view yourself. How you view yourself in turn depends on whose opinion of yourself you listen to. The person whose opinion carries most weight with you is the opinion of your inner adult. In other words, how you feel about yourself directly depends upon how your inner adult feels about you and treats you and this is what this chapter is all about changing.

So now consider your inner adult's all-important opinion of you, based on how he's been treating you over these past weeks. As you take stock of this you reason that:

- Well, my inner adult listens to me – so I'm worth listening to.
- He or she respects me – so I'm worth respecting.
- He or she treats me with consideration – so I am worth being considered.
- He or she trusts me – so I am trustworthy.
- He or she values me – so I am valuable!

And these are the qualities that you now begin to internalise about yourself instead. You truly begin to feel worthy of respect, consideration and trust. Moreover, to feel inherently valuable is to feel that you have self-worth. Self-worth is the building block of self-esteem and self-confidence. If you can already imagine feeling this way in the near future, then this is a taste of what the future holds for you if you continue to apply these ten powerful steps. Just a few weeks of fairly consistent application is all that is needed. You will have lapses and old habits rearing their head from time to time. That's okay, that's going to happen because it happens to everyone. You acknowledge the slip, apologise, forgive yourself and resume the good work. What's important is that your heart is in the right place. Your inner child is more interested in your sincerity and intent, not a perfect scoreboard.

Conclusion

Self-parenting will massively improve your emotional and psychological well-being because it is a system for understanding, discerning and meeting your physical and emotional needs.

Each step also fosters empathy, understanding, acceptance, trust, security, self-esteem and self-assertiveness. Clarification and validation allows otherwise disruptive feelings to be processed quickly, reducing needless conflict, tension and disruption. This means you are more at peace with yourself, you are calmer, more accepting, more content, tolerating the imperfections of yourself and others around you better and probably experiencing physical changes such as sleeping better or feeling lighter, less tense or as if a weight has been lifted from your shoulders.

Crucially, self-parenting is also the key to effective and lasting inner confidence.

Self-worth, self-esteem and self-confidence all depend on what opinions about yourself you have internalised from those around you in your formative years. The inner adult adopts these opinions and replays as role models and acts them out on the inner child. In other words if your parents told you 'you are stupid' then your inner adult will take up the mantle and start telling your inner child the same thing. The inner child will then internalise the underlying feeling of 'I am stupid'.

Many years later as an adult you will still fundamentally

emotionally *feel* the same way even if you have demon-strated remarkable intelligence. You still feel that you are stupid because you will not have changed what you have internalised about yourself. Your inner adult continues to think of you as stupid and still treats you in that way. Your adult explains that you're not intelligent, just 'lucky' to get this much success so far.

Note that during this time, the inner adult can think that of itself as intelligent but this won't be enough to change the way you feel about yourself. For the conscious mind or inner adult to esteem itself is not enough. I've worked with many people who tell me that intellectually they *know* they are bright, attractive and proficient at their job, but who still feel unconfident in all those respects. True confidence comes from the emotional self or subconscious mind. We need to esteem it so that it can learn to esteem itself.

Note also that if the inner child gives up trying to gain confidence from its own inner adult and depends on the opinions of others instead, any attempts at building confi-dence is doomed. This kind of confidence is a fickle and transient thing. Its roots can never develop and take hold. True confidence is *self*-confidence, not *other*-confidence. Self-confidence is all about what you have internalised about yourself and how you then project these internalisa-tions to those around you. It means the inner adult changes its tune towards the inner child, so the inner child feels dif-ferently about itself, internalises positive opinions about itself and, because this esteem is generated 'at source', the roots can really take hold, set and become permanent.

Self-confidence also means that you have trust, respect and esteem for all your *selves*; not only does the inner adult fundamentally like and accept the inner child, but the inner adult likes itself and the inner child likes itself too. True confidence is global and holistic. It has integrity and it is integrated into all the parts.

So at the end of this chapter, you have a choice to make. You are in a relationship with your emotional self whether you like it or not, so you might as well choose to make it a good one and use the principles outlined in this chapter to make it as healthy and constructive as possible. Occasionally I meet patients who want me to simply hypnotise them to have this inner healthy self-esteem without actually wanting to undertake any of the necessary work. It's as if the inner adult only sees the unhappiness of the inner child as an inconvenience and just wants a 'magic pill' to make it go away. I tell them that if they want all the benefits of true, healthy self-esteem and confidence, they've got to be pre-pared to work on their internal relationship. I can't parent someone else's child for them to make them a better parent, any more that I can make you grow muscles or lose weight by going to the gym for you.

There is a saying 'As you change your internal universe, you change your external one'. Self-parenting is a process that allows you to change your internal universe and the results have ripple effects on your external world, just as they did with mine. As you project a loving and lovable new 'you' to the world, the world will start to reflect it back.

4

Working with Specific Problems Caused by Your Inner Child

'Patients are patients because they are out of rapport with their own unconscious mind.'

– Milton Erickson

THERE ARE CERTAIN CONFLICTS BETWEEN THE INNER adult and inner child, which in turn lead to the manifestation of certain kinds of problems. These are: insecurity, self-esteem and self-worth problems; eating disorders such as bulimia and anorexia; some forms of anxiety; and unresolved emotional feelings of sadness, anger, fear, hurt and guilt, which themselves in turn often lead to depression, anger issues or other anxiety disorders. Conflicts between the inner adult and inner child tend also to be responsible for most forms of core relationship problems.

In this chapter I will give you a brief overview of how the quality of the relationship between your inner adult and inner child could be creating some of these problems for you in your life and some general tips on how to go about addressing them.

Self-esteem problems

Self-esteem problems are the equivalent of the primary colours from which all other colours are derived. Self-esteem problems, in one form or another, underlie most of the other issues caused by the emotional self, so you will see the issue of self-esteem popping up frequently in the backgrounds of the problems I'll be describing in this chapter.

Self-esteem itself is, as you've realised by now, derived from the inner adult (conscious mind) positively esteeming its inner child (subconscious, emotional mind).

You will see parallels of this relationship if you look at most secure and confident children around you. They will have experienced some or all of the parenting techniques listed in the previous chapter to some degree until they have 'internalised' them and learnt to self-coach in this way automatically.

On the other hand, insecure children will have experienced a lot of one or more of the opposites of the techniques mentioned in Chapter 3. Absent parents, perfectionist parents, invalidating parents and the like tends to leave children with insecurity around their core self-worth and self-esteem.

The key to healthy self-esteem and confidence lies in self-acceptance, self-trust and self-worth. The ten steps described in Chapter 3 have covered how to build this trusting relationship between the two minds in detail.

The passive insecure inner child

People with low self-esteem tend to seem unfailingly pleasant and appeasing, which may sound like a desirable quality but in fact hides deeper problems. In reality, what is actually happening is that passive people are pleasing others at great personal cost to themselves. They are suppressing their own authentic feelings and emotions about matters (especially negative emotions such as anger) in order to not upset the person they are trying to please. However, denial of undesirable emotions does not make them disappear – it just suppresses them. As I've been saying throughout this book, emotions hate to be suppressed and they will resist all attempts to block their authentic expression, which ironically means even more energy is needed to keep suppressing them and that takes a serious toll on the body. Research is increasingly showing that it is these qualities of suppressing authentic emotions which predispose a person to developing cancer. So raising low self-esteem is not just a 'feel good' affair, it can help with lifting physical health too. Training a person to get in touch with their feelings and express them authentically, and therefore to become more assertive and to stand up for their needs, could actually save lives.

The overly esteemed inner child

After hearing of the benefits of healthy self-esteem, it may come as a surprise to you to learn that there is such a thing as having too much of it. This, I suspect, is because the cases of low self-esteem massively outweigh those of excessive self-esteem, giving the general impression that we could all do with more. But, in actual fact, quite a few people could benefit from having their esteem taken down a peg or two. For example, when interviewed about their aggressive social conduct towards others, many delinquents and vandals reported thinking of themselves as pretty cool and felt they were better than the people they bullied.

If every day your parents tell you or indicate to you in some way that you are better than others, that others are inferior to you, that you belong to a different class of person than those around you, then you are being trained into an 'us and them' mentality. Excessive self-esteem leads to arrogance, vanity, narcissism, a sense of superiority, elitism, inhumanity and cruelty. Much cruelty comes from dehumanising others because we believe we are superior to them and they don't merit same rights as us. A balance of self-esteem is the key.

Anxiety stemming from insecurity

Most core anxiety problems are a by-product of insufficient self-esteem and confidence. Insecure children will have different types of anxieties about things, such as whether they are good enough, whether others will like them, whether they will make the right decision, whether the future will be all right and so on.

Our anxiety goes away when someone we trust reassures

us that our fears will not come to pass because they know what to do to address our concerns.

Our anxiety remains when we are either not reassured or we don't trust the person trying to reassure us.

If you have problems with this area, the techniques outlined in the previous chapter will help build that trust between the conscious and subconscious mind so that the inner child can feel secure in the knowledge that it is safe and its needs are looked after by its inner adult – your conscious mind.

Eating disorders

Most people with bulimia and anorexia have some underlying self-esteem problem, and many people with bulimia and anorexia tend to be overachievers, which also stems from underlying self-esteem issues. It's as if the inner child grew up feeling it was not good enough to be accepted as is, but needs to do things to ensure that it is accepted. For young girls, making themselves more acceptable to others mostly takes the form of doing something about their looks, because looks are emphasised more for girls than boys by parents, media, peer groups etc., and that's why young girls go down the route of eating disorders more than boys.

A fear of putting on undesirable weight kicks off an obsessive soldier part that pursues the goal of rejecting food with typical heavy-handedness, with elements of obsessive-compulsive behaviour thrown in for good measure.

There is also confusion and issues around control. The inner child can buy into the value of needing to be thin, but it can also simultaneously resent others trying to control what shape it should look like. After the inner child takes things to extremes and starts getting dangerously thin or is vomiting three times a day and taking laxatives, as in the case of bulimia, it may well also resent the new pressure from those around it to put on weight. Either way it is very sensitive to being manipulated and is rebelling against a long history of attempts to influence its freedom of choice.

Most people with anorexia and bulimia are terribly ashamed and guilty about their eating behaviour. In these cases, the conscious mind of people with anorexia and bulimia tends to be very judgemental, harsh and critical towards their subconscious mind for engaging in such behaviour. The same judgemental mindset that led to the inner child panicking about not being good enough and monitoring its weight in the first place has now changed to criticism and guilt trips about having an eating disorder. This causes the inner child to panic and feel more out of control, and when it feels like this it goes for the one thing historically it felt it can control: its eating behaviour and body weight.

In contrast, in a smaller proportion of cases of anorexia, the inner child and inner adult are in cahoots with each other and both are agreed that thin is better and superior. They get smug delight from confounding all the efforts of others to influence them to put on weight and they feel superior to people around them who they see as 'fat'.

The approach I use to eating disorders is mostly based on healing the relationship between the two minds and their relationship to food, rather than some sort of graded exposure to food. This involves coaching my patient through the ten-step process outlined in Chapter 3 and then working with the protective soldier part, which will be explained in Chapter 5.

Unresolved emotional feelings – the invalidated inner child

Unresolved feelings are unprocessed feelings. The conscious mind fails to process feelings either because it is ignorant of the fact that it needs to or it actively refuses to accept feelings of which it disapproves.

In the first case, while the subconscious mind is vainly sending and resending feelings for processing for the conscious mind's attention, the conscious mind is busy ruminating (or pointlessly analysing) about why it feels the way it does, rather than just accepting the feelings as they are and getting on with it.

In the second case, if the conscious mind makes judgements about the rightness and wrongness of certain emotions experienced then it will refuse to validate and process the judged emotion. For instance, if your conscious mind believes that it is 'wrong' to feel angry, it will refuse to accept the feeling of anger, so anger remains stuck and 'live'. Whenever the emotional self resorts instead to trying to suppress (or depress) anger or similar invalidated feelings, it ends up creating a generalised depression of all its feelings because is not possible to surgically depress one feeling without all the others being affected and thrown out of balance too. That's why you can meet people who one moment can seem happy, upbeat and the life and soul of the party and the next moment can suddenly switch to being tearful and sad. If they have an unresolved emotion, the unresolved emotion is lurking just under the other layer and that's why it becomes so easily accessible.

Unresolved emotions clamouring for some kind of processing or resolution are also a major cause of insomnia – whether it's difficulty getting to sleep or more commonly broken and interrupted sleep with frequent wakings. I think it works like this: imagine that when you were ten your parents divorced and you experienced a lot of unresolved emotion, such as sadness, guilt, hurt or anger. Your subconscious mind is responsible for presenting your unresolved emotions to the conscious mind for processing. However, your subconscious mind realises there's no point presenting these serious emotions to you now because you're only ten and are too young to handle them. You simply won't know what to do. So instead your subconscious chooses to put these emotions on hold, just like taking a loan out on credit, which you won't have to pay back for many years. In fact, these painful emotions might even be taken out of your conscious awareness altogether to protect you so that you can get on with your life and focus on the other things you need to focus on in your development.

Imagine then that another ten years go by and you are now a young adult who has left school and enrolled in college. One day your subconscious mind sends you a tentative reminder that it's time to start paying back the debt and acknowledge those unprocessed feelings. The conversation might hypothetically go something like this:

CONSCIOUS MIND: [feeling anger and guilt about ten-year-old memories] Why am I dwelling on this 'ancient history' now all of a sudden? I don't want to think about this now, I worked hard to get into university, I want to enjoy myself and forget all the past.

SUBCONSCIOUS MIND: [dutifully waits for the conscious mind to enjoy itself in university, then it sends another polite 'payment reminder'] Angry, sad, please sort out.

CONSCIOUS MIND: I don't want to think about this now, I'm trying to study for my finals!

The subconscious mind tries to be patient and to postpone its message. However, it increasingly begins to lose patience when all it hears from the conscious mind whenever it tries to present unprocessed emotions for validation is: *'Not now, I'm applying for jobs... not now, I'm preparing for an interview... not now it's my first day on the job... not now, I've got an important meeting I need to prepare for... not now, not now, not now!'*.

If the conscious mind is so busy during the day that it can't be disturbed, then the subconscious mind decides that it will have to have a talk about paying off the debt at night-time when there are no other distractions. So it starts sending these increasingly firm and more demanding payment reminders during the time you should be asleep, as if to say: *'Well, it's now midnight, there are no meetings or clients around, we need to talk about your debt repayment.'* By this point the conscious mind will have forgotten all sense of what the subconscious mind has been trying to do with these distress feedback signals and sees it as yet another needless headache that it could do without. So the conscious mind continues to resist listening. Because 'what you resist persists', eventually this conflict leads to a habit of insomnia.

To process these kind of feelings, simply float into the inner adult, zip your mouth up, listen to your inner child and discern the feelings being communicated to you, without any judgement of the rights or wrongs of those feelings. Acknowledge and honour them as they are, without having to do anything about them (e.g. 'Yeah, I am feeling quite [insert emotion] about that'). As the feelings settle, you are in a better position to see if some additional solution needs to be pursued.

If feelings are clamouring for your attention at nighttime and interfering with your sleep, keep a notepad by your bedside and make a deal with your subconscious mind. The deal should take the form of: 'Okay, for the next 15 minutes, I'm all ears, tell me everything. I will write all your concerns down. Then I promise to address them first thing in the morning when I have my full brain power. In turn, after 15 minutes, do you consent to let me go to sleep and stop all the internal chatter since I've written down your messages and have vowed to act on them?'

Hurt and sadness

Children who have been hurt by those around them they value will have underlying self-esteem problems because hurt affects their self-esteem.

The sad and hurt inner child is the rejected inner child. When some children feel rejected by their parents, they assume that it must be because they are not worth caring for. As such, rather than reacting with anger at their lack of care, they end up being apologetic to everyone they meet about their very existence. These are the rejected children who respond with meekness. Unresolved hurt and sadness can lead to depression.

To combat these problems, the rejected inner child needs to be 're-parented' using the self-parenting techniques outlined in Chapter 3.

Anger issues

Anger in general tends to be a secondary emotion, in response to something like frustration, hurt and wounded love. In inner-child terms these are:

The frustrated inner child

In its simplest form, the angry inner child is the frustrated inner child. Sometimes the inner child can feel angry simply because it doesn't get what it wants, which means that in these cases anger and frustration are closely linked. If the inner child is used to making endless demands, many of which are not met, it will retain a lot of underlying anger and frustration. If this is unprocessed, these emotions will be very readily 'on tap' and can be vented at the drop of a hat. The conscious mind, as acting parent, will need to be patient and gently but firmly coach the inner child that it can't always get what it wants when it wants and that there are more useful ways of getting its needs met than demanding and blasting people.

The rejected and angry inner child

This is another version of the rejected inner child, but in this case, rather than respond to rejection with hurt and sadness, the child responds with hurt and anger.

The anger generated can have an 'active' or a 'passive' form.

The 'active' form is 'aggressive self-esteem' – open anger and hostility to those around us who we think are not taking our needs seriously or not giving us the respect and consideration we feel we deserve. Imagine that as a child you were treated unfairly, cruelly or were neglected. You would have felt angry about it but there wouldn't have been too much you could do about it against a bigger, stronger parent, especially if that parent was prone to anger. Perhaps you made a vow to yourself that when you were older, you would never put up with such 'abuse' again. So when you reach adulthood, there is a part of you just itching to fight back to make up for all the times you couldn't in the past. At first glance, these types of angry adults can seem very assertive and empowered because they are so direct and confrontational with their anger, but that doesn't change the fact that underneath it all they have a self-esteem problem. Their previous history has made them more sensitive to criticism or rejection, which makes them assume people are deliberately out to get them, when they are not. Aggressive self-esteem is a kind of communication to others that says: 'No one will give me attention, listen to me or take me seriously unless I get angry and threaten them first.'

The 'passive' form of anger entails being angry in an indirect and passive way (also known as being 'passive-aggressive'). One such person was Vicky, a woman in her mid-twenties whom I saw for low mood, low motivation and aimlessness. Vicky was brought in by her father, who also attended the session. Vicky's father was a wealthy lawyer whose four other older children were successful in their fields. In contrast, Vicky had dropped out of school, quickly lost interest in vocational courses or jobs and didn't know what she wanted out of life. In addition, she was overweight, sported a short, unflattering hairstyle that looked like it had been hacked by my four-year-old daughter and had tattoos and several piercings. Her father came from a wealthy and traditional Jewish background and you could almost taste the disdain he felt towards his daughter in the room. Vicky's relationship with her father was complicated by the fact that she was a lesbian, which her dad saw as undermining still further the status quo and the conventional relationship he wanted for her. This was a classic case of a child getting back at her disapproving father by being the exact opposite of how he wanted her to be in order to love and accept her unconditionally. Vicky kept continually testing her parents' love, almost as if to say 'You should love me no matter what I look like or what I do'. Her parents, on the other hand, felt even more estranged from her. The sad fact was that Vicky had trapped herself in this situation. She could not 'afford' to improve her life because that would let her parents off the hook for their treatment of her. She wanted to rub her parents' faces in her life as if to say 'See what a mess you made of me. Hope you feel bad and guilty about what bad parents you were.'

To combat anger issues, you will need to go through the self-parenting techniques in the previous chapter to build your self-esteem. You should also learn anger management techniques.

Quick anger management

If you feel a wave of anger building inside about a situation, practise this:

- Step 1. Allow yourself to feel the anger and notice whereabouts in your body you feel it most.
- Step 2. Anger usually carries a kind of fast-talking audio monologue, such as: *'That stupid idiot, I told him not to do that, so why did he do that? Now it's ruined everything, I can't believe he's that dumb, what a stupid, stupid idiot...'* Tune in and get a sense of what the anger is about.
- Step 3. Give that part of you permission and space to feel what it feels: e.g. 'Okay, you're spitting mad right now, so be mad. Get your fill then I'll check back with you and see where you want to take this.'
- Step 4. Check in with that part and ask it: 'Do you want to stay angry for a little longer and be left alone or do you want to talk? Respond accordingly. If it wants to talk, ask it whether it wants revenge, diplomacy, reconciliation or whatever. Usually, once the part has had its fill of anger, it is spent and just wants peace and no more fighting.

Another option is to convert the modality from auditory to visual. My favourite is to imagine directing the anger so that it forms a fast, spinning, vivid scarlet ball of anger in my palm. Then as before, I just allow that angry part to

spin or burn itself out a bit, until it slows down and stabi-
lises. Then I do Step 4.

Depression

There are several different kinds of depression, such as
reactive depression or existential depression, among others.
Depression, like anger, is not a primary emotion but a
reaction to other unresolved emotions. The kinds of depression I see that most relate to conflicts between the conscious
and subconscious mind are all variations of chronic (or
long-term) invalidation by the conscious mind, which has
got into the habit of dismissing or rejecting the feelings of
the emotional mind.

In its simplest 'passive' form, simply leaving unresolved
emotions of anxiety, anger, guilt, grief and sadness untreated
over time can lead to depression because of the knock-on
effects of leaving ignored feelings banging around in our
system. In this case the conscious mind may have even been
unaware of what underlying emotions needed to be processed or, even if it sensed sadness or hurt, it didn't know
what to do about it because it didn't know how to manage
those feelings.

In its more 'active' form, depression is actively brought on
by the conscious mind proactively criticising the emotional
mind, of which it wholeheartedly disapproves of or rejects.
The conscious mind acts just like a disapproving parent that
thinks its child is weak, needy and pathetic and that the feelings it expresses (such as fear, anger or self-pity) are
unacceptable or wrong. When this happens, the criticised

inner child becomes the rejected inner child but in this case, whereas the angry inner child responds to rejection with *external* anger towards those around it, the depressed, rejected inner child responds with *internalised* anger or sadness.

You can get a sense of this by floating into the inner child and imagining having an uncaring inner adult. Like all children you want love, care and attention from your parent, but he or she just doesn't seem to be able to give it back. As a child you take everything personally and to heart. You reason that your adult must have good reason to withhold love. It must be because you are not good enough to be loved. Most inner children then respond to this conclusion in these two ways.

Their first response is that they become sad and then depressed, because it's a very depressing thought that one must be so unspeakably bad that even its own mother or father can't bring themselves to care for them (which implies that if your parents can't love you, who can?).

Then they experience a feeling of intense self-loathing and self-anger. The children want to actually punish themselves for being so worthless and unloveable in the first place, because they have 'made' even their own parents unable to bring themselves to love them.

As for your inner adult, he or she also loathes the fact that it's been saddled with a worthless piece of luggage like you to look after and it never fails to try to improve you by telling you what you *should* be more like, how you should be thinking more positively, how you should stop moping around or wallowing in self-pity, how you should be more grateful for your life instead of feeling down about it. Your inner adult wants to kick-start you into action by giving you a guilt trip.

But, as in real life, this doesn't work and only succeeds in making you feel even crappier and more worthless, which it then gives you another hard time for. In short, the inner adult makes you feel bad and worthless and then blames you for feeling bad and worthless. The inner child can feel that if anything it tries to do is wrong, then it can do nothing right no matter how hard it tries is, which clearly is depressing.

Some depressed people even punish themselves by eating junk food as if they deserve to get fat and unhealthy or because that's all their worthless body deserves. Others use food to comfort themselves and make themselves feel better.

Needless to say, depression is very common in any of the passive conditions described where there is an underlying self-esteem problem, e.g. those who develop eating dis-orders from low self-esteem and then feel guilty and ashamed about their behaviour will also tend to get depressed.

In lifting depression it is especially important to take on board the message of moving past judgements and then practising step 3 (be a positive coach) and step 5 (validate your inner child), of the self-parenting process described in Chapter 3.

Core relationship problems

Core relationship problems refer to the problems caused in our relationships (whether with our partner, family or friends) that are deeper issues than just the minor miscommunication or misunderstanding that has led to tiffs and arguments. Core relationship problems are about the kind of 'templates' (or moulds) of old patterns of relating to others that we find ourselves performing instinctively in certain contexts.

For instance, by day you might be a CEO and a parent of two children but when you go to your elderly parents' house, you automatically go back into acting like a carefree adolescent and let your parents look after you, despite the fact that you are now a fully grown adult. Or you may not have seen your college friends for ten years but when you meet again you behave as if you hadn't seen them for a week.

There is such a 'groove' for the emotional side of our romantic relationships too. This groove was laid down in our childhood and it recreates the kinds of relationship dynamics that we experienced at that time. Over time we may 'upgrade' this basic template to a greater or lesser extent, just like updating software, to add new elements of our experience and evolving personalities. However, there are those who don't seem to have upgraded their templates even over 10, 20 or 30 years or more. While there might be any number of reasons for this lack of development, the end result is that a person predominantly acts out according to the obsolete relationship software of decades ago, established when they were a young child around their caregivers, in their romantic relationship with another adult in the present day. The following are some of the more common (and more extreme versions) of the outdated templates that people sometimes act out in romantic relationships.

1. The needy child (the co-dependant person)

As children we are all 'needy' – obviously that is because when we are very young, we have to rely upon our parents for survival. As we grow up, hopefully our inner adult has learnt enough from our parents or caregivers to be able to replace them and become a substitute parent for our emotional self – our inner child. In the process of learning to 'self-parent', i.e., to look after our emotional self, the inner child will have learnt to trust and rely on us to look after it and know how to meet its needs; the end result is that it feels secure.

In contrast, a needy person is someone who did not learn to meet their own needs. They got stuck in an earlier childhood phase when it was still appropriate for them to look to others to meet their needs at that time, but for some reason or another they never grew out of this phase. Imagine as a young child you were frightened, you needed reassurance, praise or overt demonstration of affection from your parents or caregivers, but you never got what you wanted in the way you wanted it. If you did not get what you wanted, you continued to wait to get it from others. If those needs continued to remain unmet and you continued to wait, then at some point you will have missed the phase when most people have handed over the responsibility for meeting their emotional needs from their external parent to their internal acting-parent. This means that even as an adult, you have remained stuck in your old habit of automatically looking for others to meet all your needs, rather than understanding that you are now in a position to do something about those needs yourself.

People who have emotional needs that remain unmet and who depend and rely on others to meet them are 'needy'. Their inner adult has not learnt to be an acting-parent to its inner child, so the inner child is left looking for external 'surrogate parents' to meet its needs. The problem with depending on others rather than ourself is that we can't control others. They have their own problems to contend with. They can't always be there for us in the way we need them to be. In relationships one sees that the needy person is completely dependant on their partner for their self-esteem and for feeling good. If the partner is happy, they are happy. If the partner is stressed, they are stressed. If the partner has things they need to do and cannot be available when they want them, the needy co-dependant person can be devastated, miserable, angry and outraged and feels that their partner doesn't love them. A co-dependant person will often test their partner's love so that they can get reassurance they so desperately need. Co-dependant people can also be 'people-pleasers', an attempt to bind their partner closer to them and give them no reason to leave them. Many relationships fail when one partner is co-dependant because of the pressure the other partner feels around trying to make the co-dependant partner happy.

In such cases self-parenting will help meet the insecure child's needs at its source so that it realises it doesn't have to depend on others to feel happy. It becomes converted from needy to secure.

2. The drama queen (the attention-seeking child)

Children love attention, but they fail to distinguish between good attention and negative attention. For instance, my daughter went through a phase of not eating much at mealtimes (although she always had room for sweets). Perhaps initially, she had a stomach upset and genuinely didn't feel like eating and then as concerned parents our spotlight of attention went straight to her. A part of her may have thought, 'Well, this is nice, usually Mum or Dad's attention is mostly directed at spoon-feeding my baby brother, but they've forgotten all about him and focused on me.' So she tried it again and got the same result. Part of her may have concluded, 'I'm onto a winner here, every time I say I'm not hungry I immediately get Mum or Dad's attention.' Since we are parents, the first reaction is rarely to stand back and assess the situation coolly, but to jump in and fret in case she is ill, has a stomach bug or eaten something that has made her sick. By the time we have appraised the matter with a cooler mind, the pattern is in place. So, as you can see, children will often communicate their needs in indirect and obscure ways which can really confuse us adults. We may then operate at two levels of communication. The adult is trying to communicate in relation to the surface problem and the child is communicating about a deeper need, which he or she can't clearly articulate. Because there is this miscommunication, the adult may feel that the child is being difficult, defiant and needlessly exasperating.

If this is the case with your own inner child, then it's time to stand back, stop taking the surface message to heart, float into the inner grandparent position and con-sider what the real message might be. Then ask the inner child: 'Is it really about this issue or is there really some-thing else going on? Are you scared about something and need some reassurance? Are you feeling a bit ignored lately?' Keep asking these kind of comparison questions to clarify the real meaning and then take it from there using the self-parenting approaches.

If you feel that you have genuinely listened and acknowledged the inner child's need but he or she still wants endless reassurance, then it's time to put in place Step 6 from self-parenting (see pages 110–115). This means saying to the inner child, 'Well, you could keep asking me again, but I'll just be giving you the same reply as before. I've done my part, which is to listen and reassure, now it's your turn to take on board what's actually been said because the answer has already been given. If you still insist on wanting endless reassurance then we could spend our energies there or actually move forward and do something constructive with our time. What's it going to be? How many more reassurances do you need to have that will let you know I've answered the question? One? Three? A dozen? If after that you still need more reassurances, then I may well switch off and not reply until you actually do your part too and consider my answers.'

3. The spoilt child (the self-centred person)

While the needy child can be genuinely sorry for the demands it makes on its partner, the spoilt child feels it is *entitled* to have its needs met by others.

As children we all start off spoilt, in that we see ourselves as the centre of the universe and all others as merely our staff to fulfil our needs. Then, over time, those around us teach us that we can't always have what we want when we want it and that the needs of others must also be taken into account. At some point in our development our private universe will have changed from seeing others as satellites of our whims, to seeing ourselves as belonging to some kind of community or relationship of equals.

On the other hand, the spoilt child continues to be stuck in the initial egocentric universe, so it continues to view others around it as staff. During its childhood, one or more overindulgent parent continued to act like a servant towards their child, so he or she naturally grew up thinking that this was its place in the natural order of things. The child failed to learn that it can't have what it wants, when it wants.

Imagine you are a young child indulged by your mother. Naturally you keep making an endless series of demands, all on your terms. Your mother gives in to them all. Either she is actively pampering you (e.g. even if your father tries to impose some sort of limit on your behaviour, your mother steps in and vetoes it because she feels sorry for you) or she quickly caves in when you stamp your feet, shout, yell, scream or make a scene. You quickly learn that getting your demands met is simply a case of being more stubborn than the other person opposing them. You fail to understand that other people have their own needs, which they may need to prioritise over your own. When this happens you take this personally and are outraged. You see it as a deliberate attempt to thwart you. It's an attack on the very laws of your universe. Because your understanding is that your needs are paramount, you see no problem in using anger, threats, guilt trips and emotional blackmail to get others to bend to your will. In a relationship, these kinds of tactics take a heavy toll on the other partner.

Your inner adult will have adopted the parenting style of your overindulgent parent. Either it genuinely believes that your inner child is a supreme being, which means that any tactic used in the service of its needs is justified or it realises that it is indulging and spoiling you but feels powerless to stop this habit and impose appropriate boundaries.

To 'unspoil' an inner child, the inner adult has to do exactly what parents do when they train their own naturally self-centred children. Parents remind children that the needs of others around them also need to be respected as well, and that more is gained by cooperation and teamwork than ordering people around and ending up being alone and unpopular. In particular, the 'reality checking' step of the self-parenting process is useful here.

4. The stifled inner child

Just as some people can be 'childish', others can be 'adult-ish' and identify almost exclusively with their more serious, logical and cerebral conscious mind. They value reason, data, rules order, structure and intellect, and they are mistrustful, wary or ignorant of their more emotional and feeling side. A good example of this is the character Temperance Brennan, a forensic anthropologist in the TV series *Bones*. Brennan is a world-class scientist dedicated to empiricism and reason and so routinely fails to understand ordinary conversation from her co-workers, providing much of the light-hearted humour in the series.

The result of an overemphasis on the conscious adult mind is a stifled inner child, as if it's been imprisoned in a cage. Occasionally, when the child is set free, a normally staid person can engage in colourful, flamboyant or exhibi-tionist behaviour that would normally be considered completely out of character. Traditionally, Japanese culture emphasised conformity, rules and regulations, which made Japanese people very 'conscious-minded' of their behaviour. Is it any wonder that Japan is also the home of karaoke and some very colourful and exhibitionistic performances that are the complete opposite of all this conformity? The repressed subconscious creative and emotional side of people is trying to break free and readdress the balance.

In romantic relationships, where a more 'childlike' partner may possess some boyish or girlish charm, an 'adultish' partner with a stifled inner child can come across as overly serious, overly responsible, lacking in spontaneity and seem unimaginative and boring. The partner of an 'adultish' person may feel talking to them or getting them to try new things or discuss how they feel about the relationship is like trying to wring blood from a stone.

These examples of dynamics between the inner adult and inner child that have an effect on our romantic relationships are just the tip of a very large iceberg, but hopefully they are enough to give you a sense that working on your own inner relationship will also greatly improve your external relationships as well.

As can be seen, your internal relationship with yourself is usually the most critical factor in your mental and emotional health and well-being. Your health is in your hands and by applying some of the techniques in this book you have the tools to begin to improve or even radically change your old relationship with yourself. When you do that, you'll find that your sense of well-being and contentment with life starts to soar.

5

Managing Those Pesky Parts:
fear, addictions and psychosomatic problems

'Every kingdom divided against itself is brought to desolation; and every house divided against itself cannot stand.'
— Matthew 12:25

L ET'S START WITH A QUICK RECAP. AS MENTIONED back in Chapter 1, our minds have created our parts to protect us from things we fear (e.g. pain) and to pursue things that we consider desirable and would usually enhance our chances of survival (pursuit of pleasure). Parts can operate entirely independently of our conscious mind and some of their strategies in the pursuit of their goals can often make our conscious minds metaphorically pull their hair out in consternation.

Parts have a very narrow focus of attention and are oblivious to other side-effects from their behaviour. They rely on very simple and rigid rule-of-thumb responses that can end up severely confining and restricting us.

In fact, the irony with the behaviour of problematic parts is that these parts end up becoming problematic precisely because they *always* end up creating the very outcome that they are trying so desperately to spare you from. For instance, the last thing that people who are afraid of spiders want to do is think about spiders, but spiders are precisely what end up dominating their waking thoughts.

If your conscious mind is not aware of the motivation of your parts, it's easy to make snap judgements about them and to get angry and even hate them. Needless to say, this makes the original problem worse and more stuck.

Parts are responsible for creating and running most of the other common problems we face. Protective soldier parts (which cause fears, phobias and traumas); pleasure-seeking parts (which cause addictions) and engineering parts (which cause psychosomatic problems) account for well over 90 per cent of the parts-related work I do, so this chapter is really about how to manage each of these main types of parts and their accompanying problems.

I will first show you the three stages that constitute a universal parts therapy applicable to all parts. While each part responds well to the universal technique, I've also found that there are a number of additional techniques which can be 'bolted on' to this core technique, depending on which part I am working with, which improve results even more. These additional techniques relevant to each part will be discussed after the universal therapy.

Managing all parts in general

The following three approaches constitute a general proto-col for changing any of your parts.

1. Fostering a good working relationship with your parts

As with previous inner-child work, where there are 'parts problems', there will invariably be a troublesome relationship between parts and the conscious mind.

You will need to first readjust your attitude towards any part of you which is causing you a problem if you wish to gain its cooperation for change. Getting results is not just about applying the techniques themselves but creating the right kind of fertile relationship beforehand that allows these techniques to flourish.

Luckily for you, getting a good relationship with your part or parts is relatively a lot simpler and quicker to develop in comparison to the more comprehensive efforts required in fostering a good relationship with the inner child. Parts are a lot more perfunctory and to the point.

To readjust your mindset, let's use the same meta-mirror-to-self technique and explore this further this time:

- Step 1. Consider a part of your subconscious mind that is currently causing you distress. It could be anxiety or some form of craving or addiction or even some form of recurring somatic complaint.

- Step 2. Scan your body and notice where you feel this part resides most. If you feel it is in several locations or all over, that's fine too. Just condense all these locations into one, then float that part out of you so it stands across from you. You can visualise that part in any way – as an abstract shape, a blob, a cloud or as a little person of some sort.

- Step 3. Notice your feelings towards this part of you. For instance, if you are terrified of spiders, you may be incredibly frustrated at this protective phobic part of you for having such a stranglehold on your behaviour around spiders. You just want it to go away and leave you in peace.

- Step 4. Imagine now floating out of your conscious mind and stepping into the position of the part looking back at its conscious mind. Identify with its perspective and as this part answer the question: 'What is your positive intention behind your phobic behaviour? What are you trying to do for your conscious mind?'

  Remember, parts always, *always* have a positive intention underlying their behaviour, no matter how seemingly irrational, counterproductive, wanton or sadistic that behaviour might seem to our conscious mind. This applies equally to any man or woman still smoking while on an artificial lung or to a person trapped as a prisoner in their own home because of their phobia of dogs. Your parts always think they are ultimately leading you towards some form of happiness because they operate a simple kind of emotional reasoning that supposes that if they protect you from what you consider a threat, then you would be free from that threat and therefore free to enjoy your life. So get a sense of this part's positive intention for you and its ultimate endgame.

- Step 5. Having understood and empathised with the part's perspective, float into the third position, that of a detached wise grandparent, and consider what advice you would give to your conscious mind in the light of what you now know. For instance, you may remind yourself that the troublesome part's 'heart' is in the right place, even if its strategy or method is counterproductive. It just needs help to re-evaluate its strategy and to upgrade it to a more healthy and resourceful one.

- Step 6. Float back into the 'conscious mind' and receive that wisdom. You should feel more accepting and non-judgemental towards that part of you. It's only trying to do its job in the only way it knows how. The part in turn will feel more open to considering new alternatives rather than getting defensive and resorting to its old methods.

Building rapport plan B – the 'for-the-record' technique

If for any reason the previous technique did not succeed in softening your relationship with your troublesome part, then we need to borrow a bigger gun to thaw relations between you and clear the bad blood. The 'for-the-record' technique is a one I've imported over from my couples counselling work.

Here's the rationale behind it. Imagine you've just had an argument with your partner. Tempers flare and insults fly. Your partner then calms down and says to you: 'Look, let's forget about it, we both got a bit angry. Let's see what's on TV.' Ordinarily that sounds reasonable but on this occasion you are not in the mood to be conciliatory. You feel angry about what was said. You feel stuck and unforgiving even when your partner seems to be holding out an olive branch.

In such moments, what would help you is the chance to express your feelings and grievances to make them known and validated. Then you could move on. So imagine now saying to your partner: 'For the record, I felt that what you said was really rude, offensive and unacceptable and I'm very angry that I was spoken to that way.' This technique allows your feelings to have been 'officially' acknowledged and logged (i.e. listened to and respected). An official expression of feelings could in turn elicit an official apology or at least acknowledgment of your feelings. Your partner might respond with: 'Okay, I'm sorry I used those swear words during the argument.' Having heard this, you feel reassured that your feelings have been acknowledged and addressed and now you feel you are ready to make up and move on.

So now step into position #2 (the unforgiving part's perspective). Tune into its feelings and express those feelings starting with the phrase 'For the record'. Then step back into position #1 (the conscious mind); listen sincerely to the complaints voiced and reply accordingly. Then check back with the part to see if that is enough and it's ready to move on. If not, you may need to repeat the process again a few times until you feel you can genuinely listen and empathise with its point of view.

2. Clarifying your part's choices and commitment – The Choice of Two Paths technique

So you've buried the hatchet with your troublesome part, but you still need to convince it of the merits of changing its behaviour. In other words you still need to motivate it to change.

To do this, all you need do is guide it through the following process called the Choice of Two Paths technique. Again, before describing the technique, it's important to know the rationale behind it.

The rationale is that any of your parts driving any of your undesired behaviour have the power to stop the troublesome behaviour dead in its tracks. The part in question just needs to know:

(a) that you sincerely want to change and do not want that old behaviour any more;

(b) that far from leading you towards happiness, it is actually going to make your life more miserable and happiness involves change.

MOTIVATION AND CHANGE

Consider something that you feel you have a seeming inability to resist or stop doing; something you know you ought to not do, but against your better judgement you keep doing it.

It might be that you smoke when you know that smoking is harmful and can lead to serious health implications.

It might be overindulgence in food such as chocolate,

biscuits or other sugary, fattening products that could lead to diabetes or other obesity-related illnesses.

It might be an aversion to something like spiders or germs or vomit that severely restricts your freedom of movement and makes you a virtual prisoner in your own home.

But you can stop anything if you have sufficient drive to do so. You may lack the necessary motivation and commitment to stop smoking to save your own life because you don't value your own health enough, but what if the life of someone you loved was on the line? What if, in some bizarre way, someone dear to you was kidnapped and you were told that unless you stopped smoking immediately and for ever then that person you loved would be grievously hurt or killed?

Would you sit there debating whether you had the necessary commitment? Would there be any hesitation? Of course not: you'd instantly be prepared to do whatever it took to ensure the welfare of your loved one, you would agree to any sacrifices or terms placed on you and you would keep your commitment. What's happening inside is that you have connected to higher values (the survival of loved ones) that carry more 'charge' and power than lesser values. When activated, these higher values have the power to instantly override all other prior considerations and priorities. Changing to new behaviour then becomes effortless and you can see it through. Suddenly, you don't care about smoking ever again or giving up chocolate or facing a fear. What seemed so important before suddenly seems irrelevant now.

These are obviously extreme scenarios that we are not called upon to face in order to change our undesired behaviour. But the point is that if you had to face those situations, you would change your undesired behaviour instantly. The capability for dramatic change is inside all of us.

The good news is that it is possible to activate this capability without being subjected to such extreme threats.

For instance, many chain smokers have told me that they have regularly gone on long-haul flights for business or for an exciting holiday. Smoking is no longer permitted on flights so how did such people not smoke for ten hours or more? While some of these people doubted their abilities to manage without nicotine and fortified themselves with nicotine patches etc., the vast majority mentioned that they just didn't smoke because they knew they couldn't, so it's as if they then just put smoking out of their minds. How did they do this? The answer is that their desire to travel was greater than their desire to miss the trip and stay at home and smoke.

In other words when they were sufficiently clear about *what* they wanted ('to fly to a certain desired destination') and *why* they wanted it (because of the lucrative business deal or because they were looking forward to sightseeing) that clarity and motivation was communicated to the smoking part and that part realised there was no option but to put smoking out of the person's mind for the time needed. It's as if the smoking part flipped some kind of switch that put the need for cigarettes out of their mind for duration of the journey.

Knowing what you want and why you want it is the key to motivation. Motivation in turn then generates the necessary ongoing commitment to sustain the new behaviour.

SINCERELY WANTING TO CHANGE

Sometimes we fail to sustain change because we are not clear about what we want and in turn that lack of clarity is filtered down to the part running the problematic behaviour and dilutes its efforts.

For instance, if the smoking part has demonstrated that it can stop smoking on a long-haul flight if it really wants to, then why doesn't it just apply that same power to stop at any time? Why wait for a long-haul flight? Why does it force a smoker who wants to stop smoking to spend a couple of hundred pounds for therapy when he or she has already demonstrated they can stop smoking if they really want to?

I believe the reason for this is that it's easy to be highly motivated and clear about specific, short-term goals, like not smoking for the duration of a flight or to resist temptation and lose weight for a wedding in a few months' time or in preparation for going to the beach on a summer holiday. After those events have been and gone, motivation takes a sharp nosedive and they go back to the old behaviour. Inside these individuals there is an implicit understanding that they can put up with necessary deprivation because it will only be for a short while, i.e., they are spared from having to really change for good. They will achieve their short-term goal, they will look great on the beach and then afterwards they can return to their old comfort zones and avoid the stress of real change. Permanent change requires a lifestyle change and that's a very different beast altogether.

If the same people who can successfully change their behaviours for specific goals are ambivalent about sustaining their new behaviour in the long term, they will be communicating a very different and unclear message to the part involved in the behaviour that needs changing. In fact they will be giving that part mixed messages. It's as if they are saying to their part: 'I want you to stop smoking because I guess it is unhealthy, although I do kind of like smoking with my friends' or 'I want to be slim but I do like my chocolate treat in the evening' or 'I don't want to be scared around spiders but I don't want to go near them'.

In other words, we are telling our parts: 'I want to change without changing'.

The part is trying to discern from your mixed messages what you really mean or what your 'real' message is. It reads the underlying subtext you have provided and thinks you are asking it to collude with this 'game' of pretending to change. So the part humours you. It responds with: 'Ah, yes sure, of course master, I understand *exactly* what you're saying (wink, wink, nudge, nudge). From now on...'

'... No more smoking. I'll get right on to that first thing tomorrow, don't you worry. Let's just have our "final" cigarette then.'

'... No more sweets or fatty foods. We'll start dieting tomorrow. In the meantime, let's have our "last" bit of chocolate cake, shall we?'

'... Absolutely, tomorrow we will conquer our fear. We'll ask around for a therapist who can treat our phobia. Straight after we fix the garden fence...'

This is where the Choice of Two Paths technique comes in. This technique calls you up on your values and your true motivation. It forces clarity upon your choices and outcomes and then it makes you responsible and accountable for deciding which outcome it is that you really want to create for yourself. The part responsible for the troublesome behaviour then understands what you really want it to do and what you require of it. Finally, the technique educates the part responsible in considering alternative methods of achieving happiness rather then believing it had no other choice but to make its master smoke, overindulge or be afraid of things.

The Choice of Two Paths Technique

- **Step 1.** Scan your body and locate a part of you running a troublesome behaviour.

- **Step 2.** I'm going to ask that part of you to imagine a choice of paths awaits it. A path to the left and a path to the right.

  The path to the left represents your virtual future life, 5, 10, 15 or 20 years down the line, where there has been no change to your behaviour.

  The path to the right represents your virtual future for the same amount of time but one where your part has agreed to change and to adopt new methods and strategies for helping you.

  I'm going to ask that part of you to have a virtual experience of trying out both of those futures to gauge how it can help you best.

- **Step 3.** Turn and face the left path first. It's best to actually physically walk out over this path rather than just imagining it if you can. As you walk into this virtual future, imagine what life will be like in this future in terms of your health, your wealth, your relationships and any other related aspect of your life if this undesired behaviour were to continue unchecked. At the end of 20 years, stop, turn around, look over the path you just took and take a global overview of it. What is your overall feeling here about this path? Is it fair to say that over time everything gets worse and you end up being miserable on this path (or even dead?)

- **Step 4.** In the light of what you now know and feel about this future, what advice would the future you at the end of the left path give to the present you? The present you is not connected to the long-term consequences of his or her behaviour but only to immediate gratification in the here-and-now. Perhaps he or she thinks: 'What's the harm in one little cigarette, I'm still young' or 'Why shouldn't I have some more cake if I want to' or 'I'm afraid of the effort I think will be needed to change' or 'I do want to change and I promise to get round to it one day'. Consequently the current/younger you has been giving the part running that problematic behaviour unclear messages, saying 'I do want you to change in principle, but not right now. Some day.'

  Imagine speaking from the heart to this younger you and saying 'I can assure you it's absolutely horrible here in this future. My health is "X"; my relationships have suffered "Y"; my confidence has taken a beating. Don't make this life for yourself. Do anything to prevent this life.'

Remember that the strength of your feelings are the fuel for the 'why' you want to change.

If you need extra incentive, imagine the effect of this path on those you love and who love you. These people need you in their lives too. Their lives are massively impacted by your presence or absence. If you have or plan to have children, there are only certain things you can say to your kids or things that they will talk to you about. There are certain things only you would do for them, like walking your daughter down the aisle, and they need you there to say and do those things and not just alive and in wheezing in a wheelchair, but fit and well.

- **Step 5.** Walk back and step into the younger or current you. Take that advice from the future you on the end of the left path on board. Let it sink in. If you insist on keeping up the same behaviour, then be prepared for the end outcome on this path. How do you respond to that? Do you agree?

  From this point onwards now, there can be no more excuses for its behaviour – no more 'I didn't know' or 'What's the harm in one more cigarette...' The consequences are clear.

- **Step 6.** Now turn and face the right path. This path represents a life with change. In this future the part of you has agreed that it does not want the life on the path to the left at any cost and it was prepared to change its behaviour to create a different life for you. It was prepared to give up its old methods and strategies and explore and adopt new, alternative healthier ways of trying to please you. So walk out into this virtual future and notice what life is like on this path instead. What is your health like? Your relationships? Your career? What about your overall confidence and self-worth? Are you proud of your achievements and successes?

In addition, you have spared yourself all the potential hassles of cancers or diabetes or heart diseases or other health problems. You have added quality and years to your life. So, 20 years down the line, stop, turn around, review your life and take stock of it on this path instead. Also notice how much happier those you love are to see this version of you alive and well.

On the whole, would it be fair to say that everything is better on this path? What advice would you give your younger self about this future reality and how great it feels on so many levels to have this life instead?

- **Step 7.** Walk back and step back into your younger self and soak up the good feelings from this alternative path. How does the part of you respond to this outcome? Does it agree to pursue this right path and do whatever it takes to manifest this reality? Is it excited and motivated yet?

- **Step 8.** The Choice. Imagine I am standing in the middle of both paths at the end of 20 years, facing you with each of my palms outstretched towards each path. What path will you take?

You've now seen for yourself both futures and the consequences of your actions. A choice of paths awaits you and now you can make an informed decision about which path you are prepared to invest in. If you don't mind all the side-effects of smoking or eating fattening foods and are prepared to take the risks, then by all means choose the path to the left in a guilt-free way. At least enjoy the vices before the consequences catch up with you. Just be honest with yourself.

If on the other hand, you are not happy with that life, then what are you prepared to do to make things different? After all, you can't have the behaviour of one path and the results of the other. You've got to make a choice and a commitment. It's up to you, but you are now clearer on what you want and why you want it.

If you have chosen the right path and the reason why you want that path is strong enough, then you will naturally engage your motivation and ongoing commitment to the right path. I'd like you to formally commit to this path and take a solemn internal vow:

> 'I commit to the right path and I am prepared to do
> whatever is compatible with this path.'

This gives the part of you running the old undesired behaviour a clear and unambiguous message to change.

Now imagine that on the count of three you will focus all your intention and energies on that right path for you. Imagine that the right path moves to the centre of your vision, while the other path will dissolve and melt away.

Ready... 1... 2... 3... focus all your intention and energies on the right path, make that path move to your centre and make it bright, sunny, colourful, attractive, with the sound of laughter. See yourself smiling and being happy around your family and friends, being proud of yourself for taking matters in your own hands to create the best life for yourself and those you care about.

Well done, you've given yourself (and others who love you) the best gift possible.

3. Universal parts therapy

So, up to now with the previous approaches so far, you have:

- healed up any bad blood with the part of you running the old troublesome behaviour;
- cultivated a good working relationship with your part;
- succeeded in motivating it;
- convinced it of the merits of changing its behaviour.

Often these four things can create the change needed, but the final process for managing parts (rather aptly called 'parts therapy') is a formal way of laying to rest an old strategy and adopting a new one.

- **Step 1.** Tune into the part that wants to change its behaviour again.

- **Step 2.** Offer an apology for having misjudged and misunderstood the part's intention behind its problematic behaviour and show it some gratitude for all its efforts in trying to serve you in some way in the past e.g.: 'Sorry for having misjudged you all these years, I didn't realise you were doing your job and your heart was always in the right place. I'm grateful for you trying to help me, despite all my criticism and abuse.'

- **Step 3.** Ask the part if it would be willing to explore new ways of protecting or helping you that are even more resourceful and productive than its old methods. These new ways would satisfy the part's same positive intention for you, but just using different tactics and strategies.

By this point, getting any 'no' response from that part would be extremely unusual as you have taken all the appropriate measures to induce your part to agree. So if the part were to reply with 'no', rerun the steps in this chapter and ask it 'What measures or reassurances do you need in place in order to let go of this way of protecting and agree to do something else?' Address whatever concerns it brings up to the best of your ability until the part agrees to change methods.

- **Step 4.** Once the part has agreed to change, ask it to tune in and access the wisest, most creative part of your mind to generate even better, more effective solutions together.

- **Step 5.** Ask these two parts working together to review the best of those alternatives and then to pick the best ones and implement them in place of the old ones. Feel the handing over of the old methods to the new, like a ceremonial passing of the baton.

Working with specific problems

Although the previous three-step protocol forms the basis of a universal parts therapy package for treating the problems of all your parts, from time to time additional considerations need to taken into account relative to the specific part running the problem and so for this reason it's useful to understand each type of part a little bit better.

Soldier parts – fears, phobias and traumas

Soldier parts are responsible for generating all forms of worry and fear associated with survival (i.e. fear related to perceived threats to our physical safety). As such, they are responsible for all our avoidant and phobic behaviour, including:

- all post-traumatic stress disorders (PTSD)
- generalised anxiety
- performance anxiety
- worry
- obsessive compulsive anxiety (OCD)
- protective anger (when our boundaries are trespassed on by others)
- protective denial (reduces anxiety by allowing people to deny or distort news that makes them anxious.

This is a very long list, so taking this all into account, of all the parts mentioned, soldier parts are the most involved in our mental health problems because safety from something that can kill us is our most basic priority. The need for safety is at the very base of our pyramid of physical and emotional needs and it won't be possible to rise up and focus on other needs up the pyramid until issues of safety have been dealt with first.

To get a sense of how soldier parts operate and the kind of conflict they cause with the conscious mind, I will provide brief cases studies of the most common conditions:

PHOBIAS

Phobias are a state of unfounded fear or dread which arouse a state of panic. It's worth noting that patients seem to get most infuriated and exasperated with soldier parts that are driving phobias, PTSD and OCD because these parts can seem incredibly stubborn and resistant to all attempts at reason. When soldier parts are 'locked' onto a perceived threat, they are indeed immune to all attempts to talk them out of it by force. The conscious mind in turn gets stuck in a well of righteous indignation and judgement and loses all desire to 'talk nice' with what it sees as such intransigent and idiotic aspects of its personality and just wants that part to 'get out'.

So if you are working with your phobias, PTSD or OCD, then extra special care needs to be paid to Step 1 of the general protocol (see pages 184–187) in order to heal up the relationship or bad blood between the critical and hostile conscious mind and the soldier part.

Case study: Chris's phobia

I worked with Chris on the BBC3 programme *The Panic Room*. Chris had an extreme phobia of wasps and bees. When I saw him, he was a 40-year-old successful manager in a company. He was a body-builder and described himself as a very confident person, having appeared on several TV game shows, performing in front of millions of viewers. There was one exception

---

to his confidence and that was that he was petrified of wasps and bees.

Let's look at it from his protective part's point of view.

Your 'boss', Chris, is just eight years old and up on a ladder in the loft and comes across a wasps' nest. He is stung a few times and nearly falls off the ladder and could have been severely hurt, possibly even killed. At that moment when Chris was scared to death, his subconscious mind went to red-alert status and you were brought into being. Whenever there's a matter of basic survival at stake, it's as if the 'internal military' immediately come in and impose martial law. They re-evaluate the threat of wasps and decide that they constitute a clear and present danger. The reasoning is: 'wasps (and for that matter all similar wasp-shaped things, like bees) lead to potential death'. You, a protective soldier part, is then assigned to be on the look out for the re-emergence of the enemy.

A couple of decades go by and your boss, Chris, has grown into a big strong man who could easily endure the pain of a few wasp stings, but you as the soldier part don't care. You've been assigned a job to do and you will do it. It's not for you to question orders and jeopardise everyone's survival by taking the initiative and thinking for yourself. Chris's conscious mind frequently berates you to 'stop being a sissy, stop being so stupid and childish'. It moans at you: 'Why is my wife having to remove a wasp from the kitchen while I cower in the corner like a big fat coward?' For your part, since you have only been doing your duty diligently for the past 32 years, you feel hurt that your efforts have not been appreciated but you remain loyal to your orders. You will not desert your post. The harder your conscious mind, Chris's wife, friends or therapists try to reason with you, shame you, embarrass you, bully you to leave your post, the harder you have to fight back, because you are determined to see your duty through, regardless of the costs.

Then one day, Chris's conscious mind asks to speak to you and tells you: 'I'm sorry. I've only just realised that all these years you weren't just trying to make my life difficult and embarrass me. I've realised you had a job to do and your job is just as valid and important as the job of any of my other parts. Sorry for judging you and not appreciating all you've been through on my behalf, even in the face of all my harsh criticism.' This gets your attention and you start listening. The conscious mind continues: 'And while I appreciate your positive intention, I'd like you to know that the old protective response is causing problems in other areas of my life and holding me back. It's as if you are winning a battle but ending up losing the war. I need you to defend elsewhere in more strategic positions. It's possible for you to continue to work for my protection but in more discerning, economical and resourceful ways.'

If you were this soldier part, would you be motivated to change if you were treated like that? I expect so.

OBSESSIVE-COMPULSIVE DISORDERS (OCD)

There are many different kinds of OCD (excessive cleaning, counting, checking or pulling out one's hair). OCD comes from childhood insecurity, some unmet need or reassurance about a critical episode during a formative time in our lives. Whereas phobic soldier parts act to protect against very specific threats (such as animals or objects), the anxiety running OCD behaviour tends to be more vague and generalised. Consequently, it's harder to switch off OCD-type anxiety. It's almost always there in the background, which means that the neural pathways for OCD have been thoroughly strengthened and reinforced and therefore it tends to take a far bigger toll on the 'user' than someone suffering from a simple phobia. Since OCD soldier parts can be even more anxious and fixated than phobic parts, they need to be handled with even more patience and reassurance. Whereas most phobias can be treated in a single session, OCD behaviours tend to need several sessions of reinforcement for alternative behaviours to begin to take effect.

Here's an illustration of childhood anxiety leading to OCD.

Case study: Janie's soldier part

Janie is a pretty woman in her early thirties who came to see me for compulsive hair-pulling. She was plucking out her hair to such a noticeable extent that it was completely spoiling what would otherwise have been glorious long, red hair. Even when she had to cut short her hair to even it out, she still felt compelled to pluck out her hair.

Why would anyone want to voluntarily reduce their attractiveness? It turns out that Janie was the youngest and prettiest of six siblings, all girls except for one brother. Janie was resented by her siblings for being the cutest new kid on the block and experienced intense periods of loneliness and rejection from the very same people she looked up to and wanted to belong with. Later on, in her early twenties, Janie experienced further rejection from her siblings when she left the family farm in Australia to go travelling and made good progress in her television career.

As far as her protective soldier part was concerned, it had learnt that success led to 'open retaliation, criticism and rejection'. The soldier part's solution was to pluck out Janie's hair to make her less attractive. For soldier parts, making sure that their host is accepted and loved by their family unit is seen as one of their highest priorities. It goes back to survival – we are helpless and dependant on our family to look after us when we are young or we'll perish. All other needs are seen as being subservient to this goal so, in comparison, sacrificing looks to ensure acceptance is seen as an acceptable cost.

Parts therapy had to be done several times to keep re-integrating the OCD soldier part back with the rest of her subconscious mind.

PERFORMANCE ANXIETY AND INTER-PARTS CONFLICTS

Soldier parts frequently interfere with the work of other parts (*inter*-part conflicts). For instance, soldier parts often interfere with the work of engineer parts and this forms the basis of a lot of anxiety with regards to the body having to perform in any way. For example, I work with a lot of men who've experienced performance anxiety when it came to getting an erection when having sex with their partner.

Usually what happens in these cases is that before or during sex, something distracting happens which throws the man's concentration off, making him lose his erection. This is very normal and extremely common for all men and most men just start over again and the anxiety is soon forgotten. However, some men get very anxious and worry that their partner must be judging them harshly or they feel responsible if their partner takes the loss of erection personally. My patients then panic because they fear that they won't know how to handle these misunderstandings.

When this happens it's as if the fear levels of my patients reach DEFCON 4 – the level of fear where the subconscious 'military' steps in to take over matters. I remind these patients that the engineering parts responsible for creating the technical know-how for an erection always knew how to do their job and still do. Knowing how to get an erection and make little babies is knowledge that's been hard-wired into us through millions of years of evolution, so worrying that our engineer parts have forgotten how to do it undermines them. Nevertheless, for these patients it's the equivalent of their soldier parts just barging uninvited into the office of engineering parts and wanting to take over and control matters to ensure there are no further failures. The soldier parts are trying to tell the engineering parts how to do their job and I'm sure you've experienced for yourself that whenever laypeople try to tell experts in the field how to do their jobs, the outcomes end up even worse than before. The engineer parts can't do their job because they now have these soldier parts acting as 'backseat drivers' (when they don't even have a driving licence themselves). As anyone who has experienced a backseat driver knows, their attempts to help you drive better actually makes you into a worse driver because you are more distracted and tense.

So sex soon stops becoming a playful, spontaneous and fun experience into one with performance objectives, inner tension and worry, so it's no wonder that the engineer part in charge of sex just wants to quit.

Parts therapy here simply involves getting the soldier parts to have a meeting with the engineer parts. The engineer parts tells the over-controlling soldier parts that they already know how to do their job, so just get off our backs and the soldier parts agree and back off.

DENIAL AND INTRA-PARTS CONFLICTS

Soldier parts even interfere with the work of other soldier parts (*intra*-part conflicts), just like the FBI and CIA might cross into each other's territory by failing to talk to each other or to work in harmony to the same agenda.

Here's an illustration of intended protection from one soldier part leading to an overall failure to protect. Research has shown that in many survival situations, like earthquakes, survivors of airplane crashes, shipwrecks etc.; many people can fail to take sensible precautions to increase their chances of survival. Even people who lived on active volcanoes had no contingency plans for lava flows or eruptions. Some of their soldier parts would be trying to protect them from potential future threats by making them anxious about their safety, while other soldier parts would be negating this anxiety with denial because it made for uncomfortable hearing. The soldier parts that just want to reduce anxiety by putting their head in the sand forget that this doesn't make the problem go away. In this respect these parts are just like those people that pop anti-anxiety medication in their mouths at the first sign of anxiety with no thought about the underlying reason for that anxiety.

Beliefs and contagious soldier parts

The other interesting thing worth knowing about soldier parts is that they can be *passed* from one person on to another, just like a mental virus. For instance, I'm usually quite a laid-back person, but at times in the past I felt myself acting rather out of character and going into panic mode for some extremely innocuous situation, especially when guests were coming round for dinner. It soon dawned on me that it was as if I was carrying a tiny little part of my Greek grandmother with me who would act out whenever guests came round, because hospitality and looking after guests was a very big deal for her. My breathing and voice even sounded a bit like a subconscious impersonation of my grandmother. Using parts therapy, I released this 'foreign' part and now

I'm happy to report that I feel fine ignoring my guests' needs – I've gone from silver service to self-service.

For reasons I won't go into, I was raised by my grandmother for my first four years and so the many examples of my grandmother's behaviour towards guests that I witnessed during my childhood led me to recreate a solider part of her to protect me from being a bad host. This recreation was modelled on almost exactly the same lines as my grandmother's behaviour, physiology, beliefs and values.

In this regard they are very similar to the idea of *memes* first proposed by Richard Dawkins. Whereas *genes* transmit biological information from one person or group of people to another and self-replicate, compete, mutate and evolve, Dawkins coined the word *memes* to propose a mental equivalent of genes for the spreading of ideas and beliefs.

Another illustration of parts being like memes passing from one person to another happened when I ran a group therapy workshop for people suffering from food phobias (or so called 'fussy-eaters'). People with food phobias may eat just a handful of safe foods and are phobic of everything else. In my workshops I put my therapy to the test by having people eat a range of foods on offer after treatment. Rather tellingly, one of the feedback forms from a man called Oli (who only ate meat and no vegetables) said:

'...*interestingly, when we were trying the foods after the session, Doug had some chicken on the plate in front of him. I have always liked chicken, but it was something Doug had always had a problem with. Funny thing was, part of me wanted to say to him, "What's wrong with you, just eat it, it's only chicken, it's nice!"'*

If even someone with food phobia thinks the food phobia of another person is unreasonable and inexplicable, then it sounds as if Oli's critical and unsympathetic judgement of Doug's food phobia was inspired by those ignorant and unsympathetic normal eaters who criticised Oli, rather than his own true opinion.

So we pick up these values from those around us as children, but because we were kids we had not yet developed a critical adult faculty to filter such values. These values snuck in under our radar and we came to think of them as one of our own creations, just like a sneaky virus fools the immune system into thinking it is one of its own. If we were presented with those same choices as adults we would not have chosen all these beliefs and values. True choice is about having the freedom to pick the beliefs and values we want to choose, rather than second-hand ones passed down out of association and habit.

Pleasure-seeking parts – dealing with addictions and pleasure seeking

Problems caused by pleasure-seeking parts include all forms of addictions to pleasurable substances and activities, either as a direct benefit from the substance itself (e.g. a surge of serotonin from eating chocolate or dopamine release from drugs) or as an indirect benefit afforded by escapism or distraction from stress or boredom. That is, if we are fundamentally driven to avoid pain and pursue pleasure, then whenever we experience stress or tension (i.e. 'pain'), our pleasure-seeking parts naturally seek to alleviate our pain by trying to provide us with the polar antidote – pleasure. We've all felt a bit stressed then gone to the fridge to look for a bit of comfort food even when we weren't hungry.

So sometimes these parts fixate our attention on such pleasure-seeking behaviour as a form of escapism, to provide a distraction from other painful feelings we'd rather not dwell on. Other times we overindulge in activities because these parts just don't know when to stop, based on the simple belief that you can't have too much of a 'good' thing.

This explains a lot of our addictive-type behaviour towards the things that we know are not good for us.

By the way, I don't believe that smoking, consuming sugar, gambling or shopping is technically addictive because people have demonstrated that they can stop such behaviour dead in its tracks if they are sufficiently clear or motivated to do so, a luxury which the physically addicted (such as those addicted to heroin) do not have. Our bodies become reliant on heroin to function and begin shutting down when the body runs out of it. Conversely our bodies don't need chocolate or tobacco, gambling or shopping to function. These are real cravings and urges when we experience them, but our bodies are not actually physically reliant on tobacco or chocolate to function. They are still just cravings that have been elevated to the special status of addictions.

I find that, of all the parts, pleasure-seeking parts find it the hardest of all the parts to understand the overall damage they are doing with their behaviour, so the 'Choice of Two Paths' technique is especially useful when working with these parts.

In addition, I sometimes teach clients an additional technique with pleasure-seeking parts called 'Reminding parts who's boss'.

Reminding parts who's boss

Even after employing the general parts therapy protocol, it's not uncommon for some people to still experience a few urges and cravings for things like smoking or chocolate in the aftermath of therapy. It's important to understand these cravings and urges signals for what they are – a request for you to exercise your leadership and steer all parts of you to your new values. When most people experience cravings or urges, they tend to panic and assume the therapy must not have been successful, which makes them doubt and needlessly undo all the work done in therapy. Instead what I believe is happening is that the pleasure-seeking part is simply a creature of habit and routine and hasn't got it into its head yet that things are no longer being done the old way, but that a new way is in place.

By way of analogy, imagine a kind and diligent butler who has been bringing the master's cigar every day at 1 p.m. after lunch for the past 30 years. The master informs the butler that from now on, he wants an orange after lunch instead. The butler says 'Very good, sir' but the butler has been automatically providing a cigar on cue at that time for 30 years and it's not easy to forget the habits of decades and embrace drastic change. So he keeps absent-mindedly bringing the cigar at lunchtime until the master reminds him, 'No, Jeeves, I'm serious, I'm giving up smoking cigars and really do want an orange instead.' After a few reminders, the change will sink in and the butler will adapt accordingly because his master made it clear about what he wanted.

Conversely, imagine if the master professed his new resolution and the butler automatically brought a cigar the next day and the master took it saying, 'Oh well, I guess I should smoke if it's offered to me.' The butler is not going to correct him and offer him an orange as an alternative. It's not the butler's place to disobey his master's wishes, regardless of their merits. The butler is simply waiting for assurances from his master that he does indeed want the new changes implemented.

So if you have experienced your 'internal butler' giving you cravings or urges at the usual times of your old habit after you've had therapy, be patient with that pleasure-seeking part. It may not be out to sabotage you. Sometimes big change takes a while to sink in and it's your job to gently communicate your new resolve to it clearly, rather than blame it for tempting you. Remember that you are the boss and you set the agenda.

Willpower

A lot of people think that combating addictions is just about willpower. Consequently, many people blame themselves for being weak-willed when they can't come off or stay off, their addiction, which is quite ironic because so many of these people demonstrate impressive willpower in other areas of their life. Smokers for instance, have the ability to resist all the nagging by those around them to change, override all the messages from others that smoking is harmful, override the logic that money is going up in smoke and hurting you to boot, plus the ability to leave a nice warm interior and go out into the cold and rain to have a smoke.

In actual fact, using willpower is the least effective of all therapies in giving up habits and it's got nothing to do with strength of mind but with strategy. Stopping a 20-a-day smoking habit using willpower alone means that your conscious mind has to battle with your subconscious mind's agenda 20 times a day. In modern life it's just too hard to sustain that kind of energy with everything else going on. Sooner or later, during a vulnerable moment of stress and low energy (an argument with your boss or partner, or a relationship break-up or a bereavement, for example), there will be nothing left in the tank to fight off those urges any more, so people relapse. Fighting is not the solution but cooperation and negotiation using parts therapy is.

Engineering parts – dealing with psychosomatic problems

Engineering parts are responsible for any physical problems created or amplified by emotional and psychological distress and upset. For example, the following can be caused by the mind:

- allergies
- headaches
- blood pressure
- IBS (irritable bowel syndrome)

- ME (chronic fatigue syndrome)
- fibromyalgia
- sensory problems such as tinnitus
- many forms of back pain or neck pain
- many cancers (e.g. the overly placid Type-C personality who suppresses anger).

Please note that other non-psychological factors can also aggravate and affect these areas. For instance, people with IBS are advised to avoid caffeine, alcohol and other 'irritating food' because it makes a difficult situation worse. That does not mean that their IBS was caused by consuming these irritants and from lacking fibre in the diet. People can get back pain from a psychological burden but they can also get back pain from something like a bad mattress or bad posture. Physical problems can be caused by both, rather than 'either/or'. Different channels feed into the same outlet and it's the conscious mind's job to figure out what the underlying cause is and attend to it.

Engineering parts express emotional upset in our bodies very literally. It's common to find patients with eyesight problems because of things they don't want to *see*; or others with conditions like tinnitus (chronic distracting sound in the ears) because of things they didn't want to *hear*; or others with a physical ailment because of things they don't want to *feel*. The implication here is that if these ailments can be created in the first place, they can be controlled and changed into something else.

After therapy is completed, it's not uncommon to hear phrases such as 'things seem brighter' or 'more colourful' or 'clearer' or 'everything sounds calmer and more peaceful' or 'it's as if a weight has been lifted'. These are not just metaphors but literal descriptions of physical effects on the body.

In getting to know engineer parts, the following descriptions of their nature will help you to understand and empathise with their job.

The role of pain

Different kinds of physical pain are really just part of an elaborate feedback loop (i.e. communication) from engineer parts telling us what is wrong – physically, emotionally or psychologically – in our bodies. Pain is the surest method for gaining our attention and pain is also a simple way of motivating us to fix the problem so that the pain goes away again.

In theory, the system works wonderfully well with people who are willing and able to understand that pain is merely a communication feedback system and who can also nip the pain in the bud early on by being psychologically minded enough to discern what their unmet needs are and then to know what kind of appropriate action to take to resolve the problem.

In practice, the messages of pain tend to be too vague and unclear for most people (even doctors and healthcare professionals) and so most people remain ignorant of what engineer parts are trying to achieve. Either psychosomatic pain is wrongly diagnosed as biological pain (some kind of plumbing mix-up or some 'wires' in the brain getting crossed) or even when medical reasons have been ruled out, we might think that engineer parts are just being mere sadists 'inflicting' pain to hurt us for no good reason. Even when patients are told that the pain is psychosomatic in origin, most patients still opt to take drugs to block the pain signals themselves. They are focused on finding ways to just 'shoot the messenger' and make the pain stop rather than on finding out about the message the messenger is carrying.

Nowadays, it's easier than ever to 'cheat the system' – to lack the motivation to fix the underlying cause of pain at source by opting for that 'easier' route of shooting the messenger to ignore the message. We have easy access to painkillers, drugs, alcohol or other forms of self-medication to distract us or to drown the pain temporarily away. These pain-coping methods themselves often cause more pain in the long run and waste more energy than would have ever happened if we took the time to deal with the problem properly in the first place. In any case, if we continue to miss the underlying message, this gives engineer parts little room for manoeuvre but for them to just keep upping the pain levels in the hope of getting through to us. When this happens we end up drawn into a very harmful 'arms race' with engineer parts, where parts keep raising the voice of pain to be heard and we resort (and become dependant upon) stronger and stronger painkillers to try to shut up that voice. At some point the raising of pain levels may well reach such deafening levels that even if the patient was disposed to try to discern the underlying message, it becomes impossible to focus on anything other than the pain.

Engineer parts choose to express pain in different organs and body areas, the locations of which are symbolic clues of needing to listen and decipher so we can figure out what we need to work on. For instance, historically men have tended to suffer from more heart-related problems than women because men have been taught to 'be a man', don't cry and have a stiff upper lip more than women. Unprocessed feelings of the heart affect the heart. Interestingly, as the incidence of 'queen bees' in the workplace rises, more and more such women are also experiencing heart problems. Women tend to feel the need justify their feelings and decisions more than men, so they worry whether their self-expression is valid and acceptable (men simply care less about what others may think). Statistically, therefore, women have suffered more from thyroid-related problems than men, since the throat area is where blockages of self-expression and self-acceptance tend to happen.

Even people who are sceptical of this mind–body connection inadvertently use telling phrases which I think are more literal and revealing than just plain metaphorical. For example, one patient of mine with IBS (irritable bowel syndrome) was telling me how an upset she was experiencing at home 'sits in my stomach'. She didn't say it affected some random or unrelated part of her body, like her forearm or her left thigh. It was no coincidence that it affected her stomach area, because the stomach was telling her conscious mind that it was refusing to 'digest' some concern that it was being told to. The engineer parts were telling the conscious mind it needed to find other ways of dealing with this problem than just trying to accept the unacceptable.

Other common phrases I hear are: *'like a stab in the heart... like a kick in the gut... he gets under my skin... she gets on my nerves... he makes my skin crawl... I felt all choked up... like a lump in my throat (or chest or stomach)'*. We've all heard of 'physical' ailments that flare up when experiencing stress like hay fever, asthma, eczema, psoriasis, headaches, so clearly our emotions do affect our bodies.

Brilliant but dim

As mentioned at the start of this book, engineer parts are technical geniuses but they do have a tendency to hang around waiting for you to give them obvious instructions (not unlike some builders I've met in my lifetime!). Another way of thinking about it is to imagine yourself in a hospital bed, racked by some enormous pain, and standing nonchalantly by your bedside is a nurse with her finger on the button of your morphine drip, waiting for your instruction. You can barely speak from the pain you're in and you're hoping that the nurse who is watching you writhing in agony will get the hint and take it upon herself to press the morphine drip, but no, the nurse is waiting to hear clear instructions from you that you want this obvious solution.

Brilliant but fragile ego

One other thing about engineer parts that's worth knowing here is that, technical geniuses they may be, but sometimes it's as if they behave as if they suffer from very low-self esteem so that their confidence in their abilities is easily shaken. For instance, I worked with a patient called Jackie, a woman in her late forties who, having undergone some surgery in her stomach area some years ago, inadvertently soiled herself in a shopping centre car park two weeks after the operation and her husband was called to come to her aid. She became traumatised about the shame and embarrassment of this experience and was terrified of going anywhere where she wasn't certain there was a toilet nearby (just in case she felt the need to go to the loo and couldn't contain herself). Even though the doctors mentioned that some temporary loss of control in the bowels was normal following such surgery and even though there was no repeat accident, Jackie continued to remain petrified of it happening again. When doing parts therapy with Jackie, I had the impression from the feedback I was getting that Jackie's engineer part suffered a massive crisis of confidence from that unfortunate event in the car park that day when it didn't seem to be in control of its job. It just didn't understand why it couldn't do its job as usual. It hadn't connected the side-effects of the operation to this incident. From then on it doubted itself to do its job properly and needed external safeguards, like knowing where all the nearest toilets were.

During hypnosis I gave that part a pep talk, reminding it that for over forty years it did its job perfectly well and all that happened was that one day factors out of its control took over matters and then things went back to how they were, with it back at its job, knowing what to do. It seemed to work because Jackie was able to travel without fear or excessive preparation after that.

Specific techniques for psychosomatic problems

In addition to universal parts therapy, I've found two additional techniques very useful for dealing with engineering parts: making a pact with the subconscious mind and the control room of the mind visualisation.

Admittedly I always use clinical hypnosis beforehand with these techniques so that my patients experience these techniques in a trance state, but it's possible for you to learn how to perform a form of self-hypnosis on yourself so you can also have the benefit of experiencing these techniques in a mild trance when making your pact with your part. I realise that it's very hard to be in a hypnotic trance, engage in the experience and simultaneously read a book for instructions, so I would recommend that you read the following directions, adapt and customise my guidelines to fit whichever ailment you have that you want to work with, then tape your customised directions onto some kind of recorder and play it back to yourself when you are suitably self-hypnotised. Or you can have a friend read out the instructions for this technique to you and then switch round if you wish. In either case, with these ways you can focus on the experience more.

Using self-hypnosis – instructions

Progressive relaxation

Focus on the rhythm of your breathing, following the movement of your in and out breath. Then imagine progressively relaxing every muscle of your body, working either from the crown of your head down to your toes or from your toes up to your head. Imagine the muscles releasing, unwinding, almost melting.

Screen-saver induction

If you've got Windows media player on your computer or using the visualiser on iTunes, you'll find that the song is conveniently accompanied by a handy hypnotic swirl that can take you into a mild trance state if you stare at if for more than five minutes.

Candle induction

If you're not near a computer, another way to get mildly self-hypnotised is by first getting into a comfortable upright seated position and then staring at a candle flame. As you stare at the candle flame, also be aware of your breathing, taking gentle but deeper breaths until your breathing becomes even and rhythmic. Then as soon as your eyes glaze over a little bit and you feel a bit spacey and receptive, either signal to your friend to read out the instructions or hit the 'play' button and follow your own recorded instructions.

Making a pact with your subconscious mind

This is a wonderful brief technique based on the meta-mirror for self-format described in Chapter 4, which can be used to quickly reduce or even put a halt on symptoms manifesting further.

Making A Pact With Your Subconscious Mind: Instructions

- **Step 1.** Tune into your body and locate the engineer part of you running a physical problem of some description. Float that part out across from you and also imagine floating out the wise inner-grandparent aspect of you to the side.

- **Step 2.** Notice how you feel towards this part of you and also what you would really like this part to do for you in terms of improving your symptoms in some fashion. Make a mental note.

- **Step 3.** Float into the engineer part of you and really get a sense of what the part is trying to tell you = through these symptoms. What does it really want to have happen? What circumstances need to be satisfied for this part so that the part would feel ready to stop generating those symptoms? Make a mental note.

- **Step 4.** Float into the neutral wise inner-grandparent position and take stock of both sides of this relationship – the old unhelpful form of communication that was being used and what both parties need from each other to rebalance and harmonise the relationship.

Then it's time to mediate this agreement between them so that they start to help each other to mutual satisfaction.

Acting rather like a vicar instructing the bride and groom with their solemn wedding vows, turn and face the conscious mind and ask it '… *and do you, the conscious mind undertake to do "X", "Y" and "Z" to the best of your ability* (i.e. whatever the engineer part needs you to do for it)'.

Then turn and face the engineer part and say '… *and do you, the part responsible for these symptoms in return endeavour to "A", "B" and "C"* (e.g. put the symptoms on hold in order to allow the conscious mind to pursue a resolution without distraction)?'

Here's an illustration of this pact in action.

Case study: Judith's back pain

Judith is a 56-year-old lady who runs her own consulting business with her husband from home. Judith came to see me as a last resort (as is often the case) for help with her chronic back pain of the last several years. Being a successful entrepreneur and of affluent means, Judith was able to seek out the best back pain specialists in London. Test after test suggested that there was no organic or medical reason for her back pain and, so the specialists told her, the pain must be psychosomatic and that's why she sought me out.

In our first session, as I gathered information about her life in general, Judith told me that she had two daughters in their thirties who still lived with her. Judith had been overly mothering and indulgent towards them, so these two daughters still acted like teenagers. They did not have their own jobs, they relied on their parents and they treated Judith's home like a hotel.

Judith's husband wanted a tougher approach to give his daughters an ultimatum to leave the house, but Judith felt guilty about taking a hard line. Talking about the effect this was having on her, Judith felt that she and her husband had worked hard all their lives and it was time to retire. She didn't want to still be a mother to two grown-up women. Judith used words like having to 'carry them' and that they were a 'weight' and 'burden'.

I told Judith that I suspected her subconscious mind was trying to tell her that 'enough is enough' and that it was fed up of carrying two demanding full-grown adults. It was willing to put her own needs on hold while she raised two young children but now things had gone way past the call of duty. Now the children had been fully grown adults for a while, it was time for some payback – for a chance to live some of her own life that had been put on hold for so long and to reap some of the benefits of all her sacrifices. Judith's subconscious mind was communicating all this to her through the medium of back pain because, since it can't communicate using words, it had to resort to communicating to her just as if it were playing a game of charades – using clues about 'carrying a burden' and hoping she would get the hint.

Obviously Judith, like most people brought up in the old way of understanding diseases, saw the two elements (problems with daughters and back pain) as unrelated, which is why she kept overlooking the message and also why the pain kept escalating.

My solution was simple: to get these daughters 'off her back'. I asked Judith to make a pact with her subconscious mind. She, Judith, acting as the conscious mind, would guarantee to take all the steps necessary for setting appropriate boundaries with her daughters and get them to start living their own independent lives. In return, her subconscious mind would agree to tone down or even switch off the pain signals as a gesture of good faith. Two days later I got a call from an ecstatic Judith thanking me profusely for helping her to have the first pain-free and good night's sleep in years. I was happy to hear that my 'couples counselling' for the two minds seemed to be on the money and wished her success.

A week later I got a call from Judith asking to see me again because the back pain had returned, worse than before. In the second session one of the first questions I asked her was 'What's the situation with your daughters?' to which Judith replied 'Oh, well we were doing so well I didn't really want to cause any problems.'

She broke the pact, so what did she expect to happen! Judith had to accept that if she wanted her back pain to go away permanently, there was no getting away from her responsibility to stop dismissing her own needs in favour of others who didn't need to be carried any more. It was her choice to put up with them and suffer, or do what needed to be done and be free from pain.

The control room of the mind

This is a very popular hypnotherapy format for all psycho-somatic conditions.

The wonderful thing about the subconscious mind is that it can act as an interface between our conscious minds and real biological processes or anatomical objects (e.g. glands, hormones) by allowing us to directly communicate with these things using a metaphor as a bridge. You don't have to imagine anatomically correct glands secreting the correct amount of hormone for an effect to happen. You can simply imagine a machine in charge of a particular gland or process and then imagine manipulating the controls of that machine to release the optimum balance of a hormone or to make a desired change of some sort in your body. Your subconscious mind then effortlessly converts that imagery into the appropriate desired actions with the relevant parts of the body. It can pick up your intention and act on that.

Control room of the mind: instructions

- **Step 1.** Imagine floating into the centre of your body, in a spacesuit or bubble or force field or as if you had a ghost body that could go through any obstacle.

    Now travel up your body into the very centre of your brain and imagine entering the control room of your mind and body.

    The control room of your mind and body are where all the machines governing your mind and body are housed. Although there appear to be many machines you intuitively know where each machine is and what it does.

- **Step 2.** Summon the chief engineer or engineer part that corresponds to your ailment and allow him or her to guide you to the machine that controls that part of your body's processes that you wish to change.

  As you reach the machine, note that some settings are too high or perhaps too low and that they have been thrown off balance for some reason in the past.

- **Step 3.** Ask the engineer whether he or she could tell you what the problem is or if there is anything you need to know about the underlying imbalance. Just be open and receptive to even vague feedback, feelings or intuition.

- **Step 4.** Ask the engineer whether he or she would be willing to readjust those settings to their healthy optimal settings and whether it would be okay to do that now – just get a 'yes' or 'no' feeling.

  If the answer is 'no', ask 'what else is needed?' and act upon that unmet need to the best of your ability.

- **Step 5.** If the answer is 'yes', ask the engineer to go ahead and re-set those settings to the healthy optimal level and as that part does so, feel the corresponding changes in your mind and body, almost as if all your nervous system was rewiring and reconfiguring itself like a giant switch board.

The work done, focus on your breathing again, take in a few big inhales and then focus your intention on returning your mind and body to the normal alert waking state again.

Case study: Fridrik's pressure pain

Fridrik is a Belgian administrator in his mid-thirties. He was intrigued about whether clinical hypnosis could help alleviate some of the pain he experienced in his eyes caused by the pressure of excess fluid build-up.

In the session I used hypnosis and the control room of the mind imagery to ask Fridrik to find the machine responsible for the balance of fluid pressure in his eyes. After locating the machine, I asked Fridrik to summon the engineer part responsible for running this machine and inform that part that he wanted a change in the pressure settings for his eyes. Using a system of subconscious 'yes' or 'no' finger movements, the part was asked whether it would be willing and able to make the changes necessary immediately. We received a 'yes' signal, so I asked Fridrik to imagine that the engineer part brought up a large blueprint hologram of his eyes above the machine and explain what the problem was – just to satisfy the curiosity of Fridrik's conscious mind. I added that it was probably one of the many symptoms of good old-fashioned stress.

When we are stressed, we tense up our muscles, as if in preparation of a physical blow and perhaps this tension extended even into the muscles and capillaries around the eyes and just got stuck there, rather like tension in a piano wire distorts its shape. I then asked

Fridrik to imagine the engineer part explaining how it was going to fiddle with the necessary gauges and levers to make the necessary changes and ease the pressure in the muscles and capillaries feeding fluid into the eye, until it found the healthy optimal pressure settings again before they had been thrown out of balance. Two weeks later Fridrik reported that the pain in his eyes had since gone and that his eyes felt a lot more comfortable.

Now that you know the essence of this technique, you can apply it to yourself for some of your ailments too. Just as in the previous exercise, these techniques work best when done in a hypnotic trance, using the three techniques described on pages 221–222 to induce a mild trance state.

As we come to the end of this chapter, armed with this information and with some diligent application, you'll find that using a combination of such techniques will allow you to manage those pesky parts and feel confident in taking yet another step towards understanding and managing yourself overall.

6

The Choice

'If you do not conquer self, you will be conquered by self'
— Napoleon Hill

A S THIS BOOK DRAWS TO A CLOSE, IT IS MY HOPE that what you have understood in these chapters about your subconscious mind has allowed you to feel much less of a mystery to yourself.

You have become aware of other important subconscious aspects of your personality, aspects which go a great way to explaining many of the contradictions and confusion of some of your behaviour in the past.

You have learnt about the different nature of these aspects of your subconscious personality and how to relate to them in ways that create a win–win situation for you as a whole.

You realise that these subconscious aspects look to you for management, for care, nurturing, coaching and guidance and you realise that some approaches, such as befriending, work better than other approaches, such as self-criticism and judgement.

You have learnt approaches for improving your relationships with the part of you representing your emotional self and with other parts that represent all your other behaviours and habits. You now have the 'technology' to massively raise your self-esteem and self-worth and to reduce or even eliminate many fears, phobias, addictions, habits and psychosomatic pains, which will ultimately make your life more liberated, under control and happier.

Above all you have begun a path of self-management and self-mastery. Self-mastery is not the absence of emotions such as anxiety, anger or jealousy. It is the ability to acknowledge them in a compassionate way and then lead the part of you experiencing these emotions to the most desired outcome in that situation.

Over time, you will feel more confident and trusting of your abilities and no longer fazed by what you thought was something you could never cope with. The first time I had to change my baby's nappy, like a typical man I approached it as if I were doing major surgery. Hundreds of nappies later I know that no matter what I 'experience' in a nappy, I will do the job and even make light of it as I do it. Nappies will never have the power to intimidate me again. I am the master over them, not them over me. The wisdom of nappies has taught me a powerful lesson: very literally shit will come in life, but we have a choice over how we teach ourselves to deal with it.

Self-mastery is maturing into an individual that takes responsibility for all his or her traits and behaviours and looking to oneself for the answers of 'What do I want?' It is about becoming a leader, a CEO to all the various parts of your subconscious mind that are waiting to take their cue from you. If you do not take responsibility for asking yourself what you want and communicating this to all your parts, they will default to whatever habits were picked up from your past, whether healthy or unhealthy. They will lead you, rather than you leading them. The children will rule the roost rather than the parents.

Through this book I have continually emphasised the underlying attitudes and approaches to adopt as you learn about yourself: empathy, understanding, compassion, tolerance, clarification of your needs and a focus on pragmatism and solutions, rather than critical analysis and judgements as the cornerstone to mental health. Is it any wonder that these same qualities have been promoted by the teachings of the major religions throughout the centuries?

While you are the leader of the 'corporation', that is, the sum total of all the parts that constitute 'you', think of all the parts that comprise your subconscious mind as your teacher, in the same way that I am a teacher to my children, but my children are also my teachers. I teach them stuff like putting names to objects, or reading or facts about the world around them, and they teach me more important stuff such as love, the value of empathy for the perspective of another, patience when dealing with the 'shortcomings' of others, spontaneity, authenticity and 'being' instead of 'doing'.

So as your relationship with all the parts of your subconscious mind compels you to become more understanding and tolerant of them and therefore yourself, you can then begin to extend that learning to other people around you. You are able to have a new relationship with your family, friends and colleagues by making the healthiest relationship within yourself first. As you change your internal universe, so you change your external one.

The Choice

You have a choice, a choice about how emotionally and psychologically healthy you want to be with yourself. If you now choose to go ahead and apply some of the approaches in this book, you will see a big improvement in your health, your wealth and your relationships.

In Chapter 5, I told you that a choice of paths awaits you. To the left is a path where you simply continue to do what you've always done. On this path you've let your sub-conscious mind manage you rather than giving it the leadership and guidance it craves. Travel down this path for many years and get a feel of it. Are you satisfied with how the future looks and feels like to you years down the line? Is this the life you want for yourself?

To the right is another path. On this path you accept your role as leader of all the different aspects of your per-sonality, as a parent, manager or CEO of all the various parts of you that make you 'you'. You choose to manage your subconscious mind, rather than letting it manage you, just as you choose to manage creative, spirited children rather than letting them run amok in the house.

If you were to travel down this path instead, what would this right path look and feel like in comparison? Perhaps for you it's a gentler and kinder path, a path of self-acceptance, of self-discovery and also a path of more freedom – freedom from old thoughts, old patterns, of having to rely on others.

Now imagine living this kind of life five, ten, twenty years down the line. How do things look now? How does it feel to be 'you' here in contrast?

Return to the present crossroads where the choice of paths awaits you and decide which life you want to create for yourself.

The path to the left is a path of confusion, of unnecessary waste of your time, your energy, your health, of needless heartaches, needlessly damaged relationships and of wasted opportunities.

The right path is a path of freedom, greater clarity, more energy, more time to do what you really want, a path of improved relationships and of greater opportunities.

Before deciding, remember that you still have to do the work required to be on the right path in the same way that starting your own business might give you greater satisfaction and wealth down the line, but no one is going to start your business for you but you. There is help and guidance on the way, but it's still your job and your life challenge, not anybody else's.

So my question for you is, which one is it going to be?

Resources

Enquiries for Therapy
To experience the therapeutic approaches outlined in this book contact: www.heaththerapy.co.uk

Enquiries For Training
For bespoke training in self-esteem, parts therapies and Virtual Resolutions Therapy®, please contact: felix@heaththerapy.co.uk

BOOKS

The Portable Therapist, Susan MacMahon (Bantam, New York, 1998) is good for information about the inner child and inner adult.
Families and How To Survive Them, John Cleese & Robyn Skinner (Cedar, London, 1993)
Life and How To Survive It, John Cleese & Robyn Skinner (Cedar, London, 1996)
Robyn Skinner is a psychotherapist who acts like a knowledgeable parent to the usual bewildering questions we all have, which are voiced by John Cleese. It's like teaching the inner adult how to do better parenting.

WEBSITE

The Human Givens Organisation http://www.hgi.org.uk/ Talks about what is needed to have healthy minds and how to look after our emotional needs. Again, it acts like mentoring for the inner adult.

Index